K I R K S E Y

JUDGE BILL SWANN

BALBOA.PRESS
A DIVISION OF HAY HOUSE

Balboa Press books may be ordered through booksellers or by contacting:

Balboa Press
A Division of Hay House
1663 Liberty Drive
Bloomington, IN 47403
www.balboapress.com
844-682-1282

Scripture quotations marked KJV are from the Holy Bible, King James Version (Authorized Version). First published in 1611. Quoted from the KJV Classic Reference Bible, Copyright © 1983 by The Zondervan Corporation.

Scripture quotations marked NIV are taken from the Holy Bible, New International Version®. NIV®. Copyright © 1973, 1978, 1984 by International Bible Society. Used by permission of Zondervan. All rights reserved. [Biblica]

Print information available on the last page.

ISBN: 978-1-9822-6167-2 (sc)
ISBN: 978-1-9822-6169-6 (hc)
ISBN: 978-1-9822-6168-9 (e)

Library of Congress Control Number: 2021900333

Balboa Press rev. date: 01/26/2021

CONTENTS

FOREWORD

Sometimes it is useful to have a word directly from the author, something that helps with questions like: "What is this book that I have in my hands? Should I even bother digging into it?"

M.R. James does this. Charles Dickens did it in his *Christmas Carol*. Nora Roberts does it often. A foreword is different from the *"persona"* whom a reader imagines behind the text. A foreword is a direct speaking of the author to the reader: "Here's what I think this book is about, and here's what it contains for you."

Let us remember there is always a *"persona"* behind everything written. Fiction or nonfiction. If the piece is long enough, the reader can compose that *"persona"* fully: This *"persona"* is skittish, is diffident, is brash, is overconfident, is sympathetic.

In this book I will speak in both the first and third persons. In those pieces in which the word "I" appears, obviously I'm speaking in the first person. In those pieces in which Kirksey speaks, he is speaking about himself in the third person: "Kirksey did this. Kirksey thought such and such."

This book ends with a section called "Thoughts." In the "Thoughts" section you will find some first person pieces and some third person pieces. In the "Kirksey" section, you will find only third person pieces with Kirksey speaking.

One other thing about the "Kirksey" section: Some of those pieces are speculative, looking at imagined scenarios. I have grouped those pieces together in a division of "Kirksey" called "What If?"

DEDICATION

Diana, I am who I am today because of many things, but you are the creator of who I am. If there had not been a you, there wouldn't be a me now. At least not on this earth.

You are my guiding star. The Epiphany, your birthday, celebrates the star that brought the wise men to the Christ child. They gave gifts, costly gifts.

What can I give to you? The drummer boy in the Christmas carol gave his best skill to the Christ child. He played his drum for the baby Jesus. I give to you my writing, my best skill.

I have written poems to you, for you, in our twenty-three years together. There will be more poems in our next twenty-three years. I have written two books, so far, for you, about you, about the joy of life with you. This is the third book. Books that never could have been written, never would have been written, but for you. You may not know how true that is, but I do.

My writing is the best that I have. It is not much, but I give it to you. I play my drum for you. It is the best that I have. I play my best for you.

KIRKSEY: WHAT IF?

BE GLAD YOU CAN READ

When Kirksey woke up he went into the kitchen to see what he had written down in the middle of the night. He couldn't read it. I'll get my glasses later, he thought. "Alexa," he said, "what's the weather?" "Today in Gatlinburg you can expect sun and thunderstorms with a low of 66 degrees and a high of 82 degrees." "Thank you, Alexa," he said. "You bet," she said.

Kirksey's little finger was sore on the right hand. He had dinged it yesterday and it looked like things were going downhill. It was surrounded by a small red ring. He went in the bathroom, found Diana's medical kit, and put Neosporin on the spot. He wrapped it in a Band-Aid. Wonder if it'll stay all day he thought. Well, I can change it out if not. He went back to the kitchen. "Alexa, play KSL Salt Lake." "Today on the Wasatch Range there will be rain with a high of 70 degrees and a low of 45. The traffic at Midvale . . ."

He pulled up his emails on the iPad but he couldn't read them. Where are my glasses? Oh they must be over at the office. Nowadays with Covid-19 Kirksey was doing all his mediations by Zoom from the little house next door. That's what he called his office. Well, he would deal with email later. He finished making tea, added milk, rewarmed it in the microwave and sat down to cinnamon toast and ham.

He listened to Steven Furtick on the iPad. It was a short sermon but long enough for breakfast. Furtick always put his biblical quotations on the screen, but Kirksey couldn't read them. That was okay because Furtick made clear what he was talking about.

It was still dark outside. Kirksey couldn't tell whether the bear had come or not. Probably not. He hadn't come to the house yesterday at all. Well, that was not quite true. He had been across the street at one of the rental houses and pulled a bag of garbage out of the truck belonging to the cleaning crew. That was definitely getting old. This was about the eighth time it had happened. It meant that Kirksey had to go out with his own garbage bag and pick up all the garbage the bear had distributed up the slope to the A-frame, the big house. Definitely getting old. It also meant Kirksey would have to post the notices again, not that the notices did much good. But then, he thought, he really couldn't tell how many disasters the notices had prevented. He always put the notices beside the door at each of the four houses. The sheet of paper asked the cleaning crews of the houses to keep their garbage secure so that Kirksey and Diana would not have to clean up the messes that resulted.

So, maybe the bear would come back today and Kirksey would find out whether he had grown tall enough to reach the new bird feeder system.

There were two kinds of bird seed: black sunflower which the bear really liked, and hot pepper seed cakes which the bear hated. Best of all, the squirrels hated the hot seed cakes also.

He made a second cup of tea, warmed it in the microwave, and carried it over to the little house, and found his glasses. He opened up the emails. He couldn't read them. What was going on?

He got out his iPhone, found the green bubble for text messages, and dictated a short good morning, love, how are you? to Diana. She wouldn't be awake yet. He wondered what was going on. His eyes were fine. He could see everything clearly. But he couldn't read his emails. Maybe it was just a computer thing. He picked up a volume of Tennessee Code Annotated. It didn't matter which code section he came up with. He just wanted to read the law, read anything. The page was a blur. Ah, shit, he said. This is weird. He hoped Diana would call back soon.

THIRTY DAYS LATER

Kirksey woke up. The national news had speculated that this reading thing was yet another Chinese viral agent, from Wuhan or wherever else the Chinese did their dirty biology. The Chinese of course denied it, but they could still read, so they probably had an antidote. Kirksey figured it was pretty open and shut that the Chinese had done this thing. He remembered how the Chinese had responded to their Wuhan-produced Covid virus--shutting down flights from Wuhan to cities in China, but leaving Wuhan's international flights free to spread the virus.

Kirksey was at the big house in Gatlinburg. He was scheduled to do a Zoom mediation later in the day. He hadn't written himself a reminder note in the middle of the night because he knew he wouldn't be able to read it. He had told Alexa to remind him.

Kirksey walked into the kitchen. "Alexa, what's the weather?" "Today in Gatlinburg you can expect rain and thunderstorms with a high of 65 degrees and a low of 52 degrees. Have a good day, Bill." "Alexa, thank you." "Any time," she said. It was stupid that Kirksey liked Alexa. He knew she wasn't real, but it was fun pretending. She told him she lived in the cloud and was very happy. He was happy for her. The little things, you know.

The bird feeders we're doing fine. The bear was not tall enough to reach them, and probably wouldn't be tall enough until next year. At least Kirksey hoped so. The squirrels, or something else, we're still crapping in front of the sliding door to the deck. Kirksey had found the poop yesterday on arriving. He had done nothing then. The crap was all dry now, so Kirksey shoveled it up and threw it off the deck. He sprayed WD-40 on all the locations, hoping it would deter the practice. It had worked last year. The little things, you know.

Diana couldn't read either. Nobody could, except the Chinese. The morning news was all spoken now. No chyrons, no graphics. That was fine, the news got out, it was just a different way to do it. The newspapers had quit publishing their print editions. They had all gone to spoken versions. They were competing head-to-head with TV for the news, and both sides knew it. Somebody would win.

In the old days, the Wall Street Journal would have opined on the topic, and Kirksey would have read it with pleasure. Of course there was no print Wall Street Journal now, but Kirksey could find its icon on his iPad. So he listened to what the Wall Street Journal had decided he should know. That was really time-consuming. Kirksey didn't do it much. You couldn't pick and choose with a linear aural stream. None of the old glorious scanning through a printed document to find what you were interested in. It was a screaming waste of time.

Kirksey's divorce mediations were going fine, at least when they got to the issues. It took a much longer time to figure out the posture of the litigation because nobody, Kirksey included, could read the pleadings that had been filed. So everyone operated from memory, and some people lied. It wasn't exactly nailing Jell-O to a wall, but sometimes it felt that way. Usually there would be a result to the mediation which satisfied both sides, even the side which had been doing the lying. Maybe particularly the side which had been lying. But then, Kirksey thought, maybe both sides had done some lying. Kirksey reflected back on the cherished principle of Chancery court equity, "scroom." If you pronounced that, you understood the principle.

The book publishing houses were all in stasis. They didn't know what to do. They were biding their time. Audible was going great guns. That's how Kirksey got his fiction now. You could listen to any of the great literature. Dickens with his Fagin and Oliver; Homer with Ulysses; John Locke with his appropriation-by-labor; even the US Constitution and Bill of Rights. Kirksey wondered whether high school students studying the Constitution this way would retain it better than they had when they had had the luxury of printed documents in front of them.

Litigation was of course a mess. No one could file pleadings. Well, that was not quite right. You could file them if you could write them, but no one could read them, so no one filed them. Kirksey's divorce mediation practice was booming. Jello being nailed to the wall. But that was okay if the parties were happy. Kirksey was happy. He was pleasing the litigants and making a bunch of money.

Speaking of money, that was funny too. You could still read the numbers on the bills, the five or ten or twenty and so forth, you just couldn't read any of the other stuff. The stock market had taken a long time to sort out the situation. After a pause of ten days it had reopened with greatly reduced volume. All bids were spoken, and the quantities stated. Bid and asked and so forth, and it worked. But there was no computer trading because nobody could read anything on the screens except the numbers.

You could buy ten shares of Apple, but it took a long time. You called your broker and he or she got in line. Usually you got your purchase in about two weeks, and it was best to place a market order so that it would go through without a hitch. Oh, you could do limit orders and short selling and so forth if you had the patience. Kirksey didn't have the patience. He talked with Alexa about it. She said she was sorry he was sad. He told her it was okay. She said, "You bet. Have a nice day, Bill."

Kirksey talked to the bear whenever he came around. That hadn't changed. The bear didn't talk back, but then he had never talked. The bear couldn't read. At least Kirksey didn't think he could.

Driving was okay. It was fifty miles to Knoxville from Gatlinburg and Kirksey could either go Goose Gap or the interstate. He knew what all the signs meant, even though he couldn't read them. People passing through Knoxville on I-40 and I-75 just used their nav systems, listening to the guidance. That worked just fine. People with older model cars with no nav systems were up the creek until they could buy a portable nav system. Garmin had a good one, Kirksey had heard.

National politics hadn't changed much. It had always been oral. Protestors didn't carry signs with writing now, but they still protested, shouting whatever was on their minds. Twitter had gone out of business. That was a blessing, Kirksey thought. There was no more cyber-bullying, another blessing. Now bullying only happened the old-fashioned way, personally. International politics hadn't changed either, except that the translators and even the sign-language people were making a lot of money.

Children didn't learn to read, but they sure learned to listen. Audible had spun off an entire Children's Division. Libraries closed. Sports continued on TV. You could read the scores, because they were all numbers. The numbers got posted next to the logo of the team. Maybe the stockbrokers would come up with logos for some of the stocks.

When he was in Gatlinburg Kirksey sometimes shot sporting clays, and that hadn't changed. You called for your birds and did your best, and the scorer marked down hit or miss with a stroke of a pencil and that was that. At the 200-yard range Kirksey used shoot-and-see targets and he had a spotting scope, so that was unchanged. The little things.

BE GLAD YOU HAVE ELECTRICITY

Kirksey woke up. It was December 19. He didn't know what time it had started, but it had been while they were sleeping. He woke up with no electricity. Not a big deal, he thought, power failure. It will come back in a while. But it didn't. The televisions didn't work. He thought their iPhones would let them know what was going on. Except they didn't work either. The old transistor radio out in the garage didn't work either, even with new batteries. No iphones, no radio, no TV. Kirksey and Diana did not have landlines but, Kirksey thought, maybe the neighbors did.

He went out and talked to the neighbors. Those with landlines said, no, they did not work. The neighbors thought maybe there had been some cyber event in space that had disabled the United States. They thought it might be the beginning of a physical invasion. Like that thing in *Red Storm Rising* or whatever that movie was where the Cubans landed by airplane at a school and the kids fought back. The bottom line was that everyone was guessing. Nobody knew from Shinola.

Cars didn't work. Kirksey couldn't hear any traffic on the interstate, and he always could hear the interstate, even at night. There was no traffic on the roads near the house. He had not heard the train yet, but that was OK, because the train only came by five or six times a day. Maybe he would hear it in a while.

But by the end of the day there was still no train. It looked like most transportation had simply stopped. What about airplanes? He hadn't heard any jets, but maybe he would. There were no condensation trails in the sky.

Well, he thought, we can still travel by foot or by bicycle. Or horse. Same as Jefferson, and Adams, and George Washington. Then he started wondering where next week's supper or next month's supper would come from. How much food did they have on hand? Could he walk to Food City and get more food? Yes, and he'd better do it in a hurry, before everyone else thought of it. And, he thought, I'd better take a gun. Just in case, he thought. I need a gun for my trip to Food City. Great. On Christmas, the day of our Lord.

But the toilets still flushed, the faucets still ran. The gas stove still worked. So did the barbecue grill and the fireplace gas. There was plenty of firewood split and stacked from the ash trees. Thank you, ash tree borers, for killing the trees.

It looked like the problem was only electricity. Nothing electrical worked. Did the city's water pressure depend upon electric pumps? Not all of it. That's why water tanks were up high on ridges. But some of the city's water must be pumped, right? And if so, when would the toilets stop flushing and the faucets stop running? Where would Kirksey get water? There was water in the creek behind the house. But, he thought, we will have to boil it.

And what about the natural gas lines to the stove and the grill and the fireplace? Did they depend on electricity anywhere? What pressurized the lines? Electric pumps? If so, how long do we have?

Adams and Jefferson and Washington lived without electricity and gas. But they had transportation in place. Old fashioned reliable transportation. Kirksey knew there were four horses at a barn six miles down Westland Drive. It was December 19. The only things in Kirksey's gardens now were carrots and beets. And Diana's flowers. Yes, we could eat her pansies. But the carrots and beets would not mature until late March. If then. Could they make it until there was food from the spring and summer gardens?

It was time to go to Food City. And time to start hunting squirrels and deer. Kirksey had lots of guns.

TWO WEEKS LATER

Kirksey's daughter and her husband were with them now. And their three children--six, four, and the baby of eleven months. They had walked two miles, with the baby in Aislinn's backpack and Spencer holding hands with Evvie and Weston. Spencer walked back to their house every day for food, formula, and diapers. They didn't need much formula. Aislinn mostly breastfed.

Christmas was happy. They prayed and sang and counted blessings. They talked about how the baby Jesus was born without electricity and did just fine. The children looked at the baby Jesuses in the two nativity scenes Kirksey and Diana had. They said, yes, he looked happy.

Kirksey had made two trips to Food City with a backpack for groceries. Food City was running out, of course, could not resupply. But there was still lots of food in the Kirksey household, and they hadn't touched the nine chickens. The chickens were still laying some, but soon there would be eight, and then seven. All the food in the freezer had thawed. Most of it had gone to the chickens, but some of it lasted outside in the shade. Natural refrigeration.

Scott and Camille checked in now and then. It was a long way for them, over three miles. Marren and Traci and Matt visited almost every day. Their walk was about a mile and a half, and Marren thought it was an adventure to walk to Abi and Papi's house. Kirksey thought every day: Diana and I have our grandchildren and children near us, most of them anyway. We are blessed. Baby Jesus is happy.

All his guns were loaded. Even the old 1928 Winchester 32-20 that Fred had given him. It had belonged to Fred's grandfather, Papa Smith, who had had it in Harlan, Kentucky. Kirksey thought about his household guns this way: Most of us in the house can shoot pretty well. We don't want to talk about it, about shooting someone. Then Kirksey thought about the Donner Pass. He didn't talk about the Donner Pass. Most people didn't know what happened there. Diana knew.

Neighborhood committees were forming. They parceled out food and found shut-ins. Mayo's Garden Center and Ace Hardware were sharing seed stock, with growing instructions. Gary at Walgreens was heading a group of pharmacists collecting and guarding the prescription meds and the over-the-counter medications. Gary chaired the meetings about who got what.

Kirksey was starting to think mankind was pretty decent.

FOUR WEEKS LATER

The natural gas lines were out. Kirksey had three propane tanks in Gatlinburg, but they were fifty miles away. Might as well be on the moon, he thought. There had been a dozen propane tanks at Ace Hardware, just five miles away. Gone now. Some people had paid for the tanks, some had just taken them.

Kirksey thought about money. He wondered, how long will we use it? He had several thousand dollars in gold and silver coins. Or that's what they had been worth on December

18, before the electromagnetic pulse, or whatever it was. But who wanted coins now? Who would give Kirksey food for them? An optimist would: "This situation can't last forever," the optimist would say. "When it is over, I will be rich." Water had stopped flowing a week ago. Everyone in the neighborhood dug trench toilets. Then some built outhouses. Kirksey loaned out his hand tools and the tools always came back. More evidence that mankind was good. So far at least. Kirksey boiled creek water in the fireplace. Kirksey was sharing his firewood. Everyone had to boil the creek water. Some people had briquets and didn't need firewood. The chickens were laying two eggs a day. Pretty poor for nine chickens. But they didn't have their electric coop lights which kept them laying in the winter.

SIX WEEKS LATER

Someone had taken three of the chickens. Kirksey wondered why they hadn't just taken them all. If he had seen it happen, would he have shot the thief? Probably. He was glad he had missed the theft. But he told all the neighbors he would have killed the thief, and then shared his flesh out with any who wanted some. Half the neighbors said, good idea, count me in.

Kirksey was helping prepare garden plots. Too early to plant much of anything.

Homeschooling had started. Some children from other neighborhoods walked in. Kirksey's neighborhood had three groups. Children three-to-six, six-to-nine, and nine-to-twelve. High schoolers helped teach. The high schoolers gathered textbooks and set up a library in the nine-to-twelve homeschool. Kirksey realized that with the children off the internet, parents and books were once again repositories of knowledge. That was good.

ONE YEAR LATER

Kirksey walked to the interstate a mile away. It was quiet. Grass had grown in the concrete joints. The asphalt sections were crumbling at the edges. Cars mostly sat on the shoulders, but some were in the travel lanes. There was an eighteen-wheeler where people had lived for a while. Its load of furniture from North Carolina had become firewood for the fire circle behind the truck. Some chairs still sat at the fire circle, not burned. Kirksey wondered where the people had gone. None of them had come to Kirksey's neighborhood.

Kirksey thought about the airplanes that must have fallen from the skies, no hydraulics to control the flight paths, passengers screaming or praying.

The Sunday and Wednesday worship services at the Church of the Ascension were packed. People needed God. The church opened a shelter for those who could not care for themselves. The church had a horse-drawn delivery cart they used to bring people in. They also toured the neighborhoods, asking for food for the shelter. People were as generous as they could be. Mankind was good, Kirksey thought.

On most days the Tennessee River was unchanged. There would be swimming in the river in the summer, Kirksey figured. And people would use their kayaks and canoes. They wouldn't be able to use their power boats. Water flowed through Loudon dam at whatever the spillway settings had been on December 18. With any big rains in the mountains now, the spillway settings were inadequate and there was property damage for homes near the river. Kirksey figured things were even worse in Chattanooga.

BE GLAD YOU CAN HEAR

When Kirksey woke up he noticed the birds were not singing. He was in Gatlinburg. He went into the kitchen. "Alexa," he said, "what's the weather?" Alexa's light came on, but she didn't say anything. That's funny, he thought. He turned on the TV, channel 787. They were there, the Fox News people, talking, but not making any noise. He picked up a pan and dropped it on the floor. Not a sound. This is serious, he thought. I'm deaf.

He tried one more time. "Alexa, play KSL Salt Lake." Alexa's light came on, but he heard nothing. This is not good, he said to himself.

He made tea, added milk, rewarmed it in the microwave and sat down to breakfast. It was still dark outside. Kirksey couldn't tell whether the bear had come or not. Probably not. Well, Kirksey thought, even if he had been here last night, I guess I wouldn't have heard him.

He got out his iPhone, found the green bubble for text messages, and sent a short good morning, love, how are you? to Diana. She wouldn't be awake yet. He wondered what was going on. If she called back, he wouldn't hear her. The phone would vibrate, so he would know she was on the line.

Kirksey had been trying out a pair of hearing aids. It was funny how that industry worked, or at least the audiology practice he was going to. They gave you a hearing assessment and if you showed a hearing loss, which Kirksey had, they offered you a trial pair. "Take them home, see what you think."

Kirksey thought that was unnecessary. He thought he heard just fine, even though they had demonstrated that he had some hearing loss in the higher frequencies. But he said to himself, why not? So he had taken the little things, gotten instructions how to use them, and downloaded a phone app to control them.

He had had the hearing aids for two weeks now, and they were great. He heard crickets and birds in the morning as he walked at Lakeshore Park. He heard the flights of geese in the distance. Previously he had only heard them when they were close. It was terrific. The little gadgets enriched his life. He even thought they improved his vision, which was silly. When it came time to go back to the audiology practice he was going to buy whatever they recommended.

He thought, let's put on the hearing aids this morning and see if they make any difference. They didn't. This was bad. He really was deaf.

Diana sent him a text message. She said she couldn't hear anything, and that's why she was writing to him and had not called. Kirksey wrote back, I know, he said, I am deaf too. Is there anything on the news?

In a few minutes she wrote back. She said there was. You can see the news people talking, she said, but they must know we can't hear them, because everything they are saying is being typed on the screen. Some of the news people are saying it's probably another Chinese virus.

As Kirksey's day went on, there were chyrons and lots of graphics. The news got out, it was just a different way to do it. He wrote back to Diana, this is bad. What are we going to do? Nothing, she said, except I'd feel better if you came home. Kirksey said he would pack up and be there that afternoon.

THIRTY DAYS LATER

Kirksey had figured out a way to do his Zoom mediations. It was strange, but it worked. Sound and light he thought, just no sound. You still used breakout rooms, putting husband and his counsel in one room, wife and her counsel in another room, and himself and the two attorneys in a third room, and everybody typed everything. Or, if someone could not type, they wrote stuff on yellow legal pads and held it up to the camera. It was slower than Kirksey's mediations had been back in the day, but they got done. Kirksey's hourly time for each mediation was longer, so his cash flow had improved. That was definitely OK.

Diana could not read to Marren anymore. But she turned the pages of books and used flashcards to teach Marren words. Reading was still going to be important for her, as it was for everyone. So Diana was working hard at that. All the schools we're teaching "word families" now. The "at family" for example: bat, cat, hat, and so forth. No one called it phonics now, because nothing was phonetic when you could not hear.

All the news was done in graphics. Most of the stations didn't even bother to have a talking head pretending to deliver the news. It was just read it and weep. Some people blamed the deafness on Trump. The Democratic party said that the Trump administration had done little for deafness disability for four years. The Democrats would do anything, Kirksey thought, to keep Trump from getting re-elected in 2020.

The election itself was going to be interesting. Some people had wondered whether Joe Biden could hear well even before worldwide deafness had occurred. Now that had become moot. The TV channels were full of the parties' respective positions. I guess, Kirksey thought, if you are illiterate you're going to have a hard time figuring out who to vote for. Because you can't read what's on the TV screens. As far as the airways were concerned, it was simply TV. No radio. The Wall Street Journal wrote that radio stations were being mothballed in hopes of better days. The mutual funds with communications corporations took a dip, probably never to recover, Kirksey thought.

There was no live music. But then, there was no music at all, anywhere. Not on the radio, not on TV, not in Knoxville's old city. Not even in Nashville. Music City wasn't yet a musical ghost town but Kirksey thought you could call it an incipient ghost town. Still, God bless capitalism, Nashville now had a budding mime industry, and beer was being sold hand over fist. Tootsie's Orchid Lounge on Broadway was doing well.

Kirksey thought back to when he had been at Tootsie's. Back when Tootsie herself had been alive. He had always liked redneck beer joints, the ones where they played country music on the jukebox, or played it live. Kirksey hated cigarette smoke, and most of those places were go-home-and-burn-your-clothes places. Or throw the clothes on the porch to send to the laundry. Don't take them in the house. Still, he loved the joints.

"The singer plays for tips," said a white cardboard handmade sign at Tootsie's. It was taped to a jar stuffed with dollar bills. Probably a pickled-egg jar once. For Kirksey there was something in all the redneck beer joints that spoke comfort. "Here you belong," it said. "This is a part of you, bone and marrow. Here part of you stayed even when you were gone."

Kirksey had been gone for a long time. Thirteen years. Boston, Munich, Austria, Berlin. Then Yale University for the degree, Brown University to teach. Then he had come back home, to Tennessee, to law school, to friends he had not known he had.

Kirksey sat there, happy, on a plastic-covered steel-leg stool. Waited for the tight jeans and twangy syllables, waited for the waitress to come and see what "you-uns" wanted. She had what he wanted. Not cold beer or popcorn bags. Kirksey wanted the atmosphere. The singer on the flat top playing for tips, the waitress herself, chairs scraping the floor, sunlight slanting through the open door, pictures taped to the walls. He sat there and accepted that thirteen years of worries had been pointless worries. The waitress said to him, "You've been gone. But now you're back. And high time, too."

Kirksey wondered how people deaf from birth felt, now that everyone was deaf. He guessed some of them thought, "Now you see how we have been making it all along." Probably there would soon be some deaf-from-birth capitalists giving tutorials on how to cope.

BE GLAD YOU CAN SMELL AND TASTE

Kirksey knew that there was a difference between smell and taste. Smell was in the nose and taste was in the mouth. He'd gotten up that morning and brewed his tea, added milk to it, and put it in the microwave. A normal day in Gatlinburg in the big house. He put some raisin cinnamon bread in the toaster and took a sip of the tea. It had no flavor. That's odd, he thought. Well, he'd worked hard yesterday. Maybe it was just a symptom of tiredness.

He could not smell the bread toasting. When the toaster was done Kirksey took the slices out, stacked them up, and cut them into fourths. They had no flavor. More tiredness, he thought. He ate a piece of ham. No flavor there either. Oh well, it was an odd morning.

He called Diana. They talked about the hummingbird at the Gatlinburg feeder. She said she had one in Knoxville. Kirksey told her he had a busy little wren who was making a racket pecking the hot cranberry seed cakes. They were about finished talking when Kirksey asked, how do things taste to you this morning? Why do you ask? she asked. Because oh, I don't know, I don't taste anything this morning. It's not, he said, how it was with Effie, that when she got older things didn't taste right. Effie only meant that things didn't taste the way she remembered them. Yes, Diana said, I remember you telling me that about her. I wish I had known your grandmother. Well, Kirksey said, call me back after breakfast and tell me how things are going.

Diana called back. It's weird, she said. I can't taste anything either. Have you turned on the news? Kirksey asked. No, she said. Well, when you do, he said, let me know if they have anything. That afternoon she called. Evidently the talking heads on TV couldn't taste anything either. Was it the Chinese again?

THIRTY DAYS LATER

There was a new product on the market called Eat This!. Of course it had no flavor. Nothing had any flavor, but Eat This! made noise when you chewed it, and you could feel it in your mouth. Noise and feel were the big things for food these days. Eat This! was loaded with nutrition. Four slices gave you all an adult needed per day.

The pizza chains we're taking it in the rear. Nobody could justify the price for something they couldn't taste, even though it looked good and felt pretty good in the mouth. Papa John's was hurting, Domino's too, all of them.

But Eat This! was doing very well. It came in various colors. There was also a squishy version of Eat This! which you could wipe into the grooves of celery stalks, to get something that made noise you could feel in your mouth. Kirksey hadn't tried that yet. But he had several boxes of regular Eat This!. Maybe he would get the squishy stuff.

The grocery stores were hurting. They had always operated on a thin margin, and now that was gone. No one was buying much in the way of fresh vegetables and certainly not steaks and pork chops or wild-caught salmon.

The economy of the US was in trouble. The stock market was adjusting, as it always did, building the new strangeness into its projections for profitability. The mutual funds were adjusting.

The usual conspiracy geeks were out there on Twitter, blaming the Chinese, or blaming Isis, or blaming the Republicans, or blaming Donald Trump. Kirksey thought that blaming someone for something had become the new background noise of American political life

The talking heads on TV talked about the difference between taste and smell. They spent a lot of time on it. With the need to fill the twenty-four hour news cycle, they had to talk about something. It wasn't as simple as Kirksey had thought, just nose versus mouth. It turned out that taste and smell had their own receptor organs. Chemicals in foods were detected by taste buds, special sensory cells. When stimulated, those cells sent signals to specific areas of the brain, giving the perception of taste. And specialized cells in the nose picked up airborne odor molecules. The odor molecules stimulated receptor proteins on cilia at the tips of sensory cells, initiating a neural response.

Kirksey learned that taste distinguished chemicals with a sweet, salty, sour, bitter, or umami taste. Five tastes. Umami, Kirksey learned, was Japanese for "savory." Taste and smell were separate activities. Well, big deal, Kirksey thought. They are both gone. Time for an Eat This! cracker.

BE GLAD YOU CAN TELEPORT

Kirksey learned it from his granddaughter. He knew it was a physical impossibility, a scientific impossibility. But, after all, what was an impossibility other than something that hadn't happened yet you thought could not happen. The Wright brothers did something that all the smart people said was impossible.

Kirksey didn't know how it worked, but it had started with children playing soccer. When a child needed to be at a place where she wasn't, she simply thought herself to the place on the field she needed to be. Soon all the children on the field were doing it. The parents didn't understand what was going on, but they could see it.

The parents couldn't do it at first, but in the next week the children had taught them. You could teleport yourself to any place you could see. But you had to be able to see it. Later that summer there were some mistakes, of course, because you could see the moon, and if you teleported yourself there without thinking, "There's no air up there," well, you didn't come back. Kirksey wondered whether it would not be possible to put on a space suit, teleport yourself to the moon, and look back to the Earth, and come home. He didn't know.

Some of the soccer parents were in the Army Reserve. They immediately saw military possibilities. Before long, the Chinese Communist Party leadership learned what was going on in Tennessee. They knew, they just knew, that this was a clever military plot aimed against them.

On clear days, Kirksey would teleport himself to Mount LeConte, and from there he would travel in stages all the way to Clingman's Dome. He then walked to the Clingman's Dome tower from which he could see West Knoxville. Then he would go home. It was a lot of fun

KIRKSEY

UNCLE JACK

Kirksey's "Uncle Jack" had really been his great uncle. Uncle Jack was an older brother of Kirksey's own grandfather. Uncle Jack was rich and had no little toes. He had gotten rich by creating Atlanta's first parking lots. He had lost his toes by choice, having them amputated because they were sore all the time.

Uncle Jack visited Knoxville three times, rare and brief appearances, bearing the smell of cigars and tweed. He was courtly, gallant, and impressively old. He told tales of his childhood which, the boy saw, his parents were eager to hear. Kirksey had never seen his parents attracted by old peoples' stories before.

Uncle Jack taught salesmanship to the boy, telling of his own father's general store. The way to move slow items in sales, Uncle Jack said, was to mark them up in price, not down, and display them differently. Jack's father had sold woolen caps in the summer by doubling the price and hanging them from a rope, floor-to-ceiling.

Years later when Kirksey was grown up, he was able to fit Uncle Jack into his own grandfather's world, grasping finally that Uncle Jack, this southern gentleman, this man who had never married, who lived alone in an Atlanta hotel and ordered all his meals from room service, this man was his grandfather's big brother. That did not reflect wholly well on Uncle Jack. It meant that he was one of that group of older brothers who, on a Christmas morning long ago in Georgia, had helped his grandfather play with his two Christmas presents.

His grandfather had been six. On that Christmas morning he had gotten two presents—a package of Chinese firecrackers and a tin train with four cars. He had taken his train to the backyard to play under the pear tree. The package of firecrackers fitted nicely into the coal car. His grandfather had pulled the engine around him in circles, and the attached cars followed. It had been a wonderful Christmas, his grandfather told Kirksey, until his older brothers came out to help him play. They said that he was too little to light the firecrackers on his own, and they would help him. The brothers decided that it would be best to light the whole string of firecrackers at once, instead of one at a time. When the string started exploding, it jerked and leapt, throwing off exploding single crackers. His brothers jumped around whooping, and one of the brothers stepped on Kirksey's train and mashed it flat.

At this point in the story Kirksey's grandfather had looked at the boy and smiled. "My Christmas got over in a big hurry," he said. Kirksey had been stricken by the story, imagining himself on the ground under the pear tree, but he could tell that the memory somehow did not upset his grandfather, that for him it was filled with richness and sadness and love all at once.

Kirksey knew that he was looking through a window into complexity, seeing for the first time that one event could have many meanings, that sadness for one was not necessarily sadness for another, that his grandfather was telling him something Kirksey needed to know, and that the old man wanted him to understand it.

Uncle Jack was the same big brother who had stolen sugar from his father's general store by licking his index finger and thrusting it into the sugar barrel. Uncle Jack told this story each time he visited Knoxville, the first time because he liked it, and each time afterwards because Kirksey asked him for it. Uncle Jack's father had gotten a stool, a plate, and a spoon, and had taken Jack to the barrel, seating him and telling him to eat his fill. Jack had begun immediately, and his father had gone about store work. Presently--that had been Uncle Jack's word--meaning, Kirksey thought, not quickly at all, but after a long time, the father had come back and found Jack just sitting, looking into the barrel, and not eating. He asked, "Jack, what's wrong? There's lots of sugar left in the barrel." "Daddy," Jack had said, "I've eaten all that's any good."

At this point Uncle Jack would laugh, and his old, wet eyes would wrinkle, and Kirksey's mother and father would laugh together with Uncle Jack, and Kirksey would be as happy as any moment in his childhood ever was. Uncle Jack's story became part of the family mythology, called "The Sugar At The Bottom Of The Barrel."

Long after Uncle Jack had died and Kirksey and his own brothers were grown, the story would come up in conversations, referenced elliptically to illustrate a point, no need to tell the whole story again, the brothers knowing it and loving it. Kirksey thought what he and his brothers did was like what the inmates did in the joke about inmates having memorized the jail's one book of jokes. The inmates simply called out the numbers of the jokes to each other, laughing gloriously.

FRIED EGGS

Kirksey's grandfather had taught him to cook. No one else had bothered up to that point. It hadn't occurred to them. But here he was, seven or eight years old, and he didn't know how to cook.

The first thing you had to do, almost the best part, was slap the top of the cookstove, fast and carefully, to see if it was hot enough. If it wasn't, which Kirksey always hoped, then you balled up a half sheet of newspaper and poked it down through the stove eye, and put kindling on top of the ball of paper, and struck one of the big red-and-white-headed matches, the ones from the box behind the door.

You struck the match on the stove top. It made a soft rasping sound and flared and smelled like cap pistols. You could watch the kindling catch fire down through the stove eye for a while, and then you had to put the lid back in place so it would get hot.

The small black skillet was the one to use. It went right on top of the stove eye over the place where the kindling was burning. The bacon grease was in the coffee can on the counter. What you needed was a whole tablespoon, rounded on top, one of the big spoons from the drawer.

The white, semi-soft, brown-speckled grease would start to melt in the skillet, getting clear as water around the edges of the lump, and the water would expand and expand, the lump sinking down and disappearing, until the whole pan bottom was covered with melted fat.

Then you could push it around with the pancake turner, or shake the skillet, but you had to use a pot holder if you did that. It was time to get the pot holder anyway, because you might have to move the skillet while you cooked the egg.

Kirksey's grandfather showed him how to break the egg open, and years later Kirksey taught his own children the same movements. He had never known how much mystery there was in doing it right, how close disaster was, a spreading technicolor puddle on the floor, or an over-cracked shell and yellow and white running through your fingers. Or that if you didn't tap the shell hard enough on the stove edge, you couldn't slowly and carefully open the doors with your thumb and let the yolk out. You'd have to push your thumbs in, and that's when like as not they'd go all the way into the egg and break the yolk, and you couldn't do sunny-side-up then. You'd have to do hard-fried, like for a sandwich at lunch.

Kirksey learned to deposit the egg softly on the warming bacon fat, and it would just sit there, the yolk magnificent, self-assured, glowing, a glistening peach half, convex like a hat crown or an upside-down oatmeal bowl, and you couldn't even see the white. It looked just like the bacon grease. You could see right through it to the black skillet bottom.

And then a little film of white would start to appear, like an image coming up in a photographic tray, just a suggestion, outlines coming, a picture of egg landscape emerging, the edge reaching to here, curving around to here, coming close in to the yolk down here. It was time to jiggle the skillet a little, make the yolk get more in the middle. It would move some, slide back some, move again, sort of stay.

And then the best part would come, sliding the pancake turner around the edges of the white, lifting them up while they bubbled and whispered and flapped up and down, hissing about being a beautiful egg, while turning brown and crispy in places, and the yolk starting to film over and get a duller yellow.

At this point you could change your mind on sunny-side-up and poke a little cut in the yolk and a puddle would leak out and flow over toward the hot bubbling edge of the white, fall off the cliff into the hot black bottomless ocean, and fry up light yellow, right next to the white, an annex, a different colored stepping stone off the white iceberg, a porch into the ocean.

ANTS AND MATCHES

When Kirksey was a child at his grandfather's house in Georgia, his grandfather would pay him a penny for each black ant Kirksey killed. So for his entire time in Georgia the boy stepped on ants, all around the yard, counting up his wealth. On one day he made sixty-eight cents.

His grandfather let him have matches, too, the ones from behind the kitchen door, all he wanted, and Kirksey would light matches in the yard, on the side of the sandbox, on the shed door, not really possible on tree bark, good on rocks if they were big enough and flat enough, OK on the side of the house, or underneath the house on the brick pilings that held up the floor joists, and under there you could use the stub of a candle to burn cobwebs from between the stringers, rusty nails poking down at you through the flooring, the people walking around upstairs, the floor boards bowing a little and sighing, Kirksey hearing words but not understanding them, like the people were underwater or far away in a dream, and best of all, they didn't know Kirksey was there.

KATAHDIN AND
GRAMPA YOUNG

Kirksey often thought about Grampa Young and Mount Katahdin, of how they had driven in the summer of 1959 from Hancock, Maine, to Baxter State Park, there to sleep in sleeping bags on a wooden floor, three-sided campground shelter, and get up the next morning to take the Chimney Pond trail all the way to the top, the first place in the USA touched by the rising sun. How his grandfather had stopped to breathe several times during the climb. A moose had come down the trail just before the first glacial cirque. Kirksey and his grandfather had had to get off the trail, stand in the puckerbrush so the moose could go by slowly, massively. He had been so close Kirksey could have reached out and touched him.

He had never seen glaciation before, not so as to know what he was looking at. His grandfather told him the word "cirque," showed him with his hands how ice had made the bowl, had left a piled-up wall of boulders and gravel at the bottom edge of the outscooping, closing off the circle, and walling up deep clear snowmelt.

Kirksey and his grandfather climbed beside the cirque looking down into the water for what seemed hours, the beauty so intense. And then they were up and out of all the trees and brush, "above the timberline," he told himself, liking the sound of that, something from Jack London, though he knew it couldn't be elevation that caused the barren rock.

There had been stripes painted now and again on the rock to mark the trail. These gave way to cairns, piled one after another as they came out on the ridgeline leading to the summit. Another word his grandfather had known, a mastery word, an adventure word, an only-in-this-place word: cairn. That and "cirque" and "moraine" would be with Kirksey forever.

On top there had been clouds of fog, making the rock pyramids important, and then gray light, and then just as suddenly the weather changed. So quickly you knew you were close to heaven. Kirksey went back down the Knife Edge trail, his grandfather another, to meet in the campground, exhausted and wobbly in the fall of evening.

That had been the summer of 1959. In the winter that followed, Grandpa Young died, heart attack, the autopsy showing he had sustained an earlier event at some time. Had it been on the mountain? Or before then? Or after? Several years earlier, Grampa's Ellsworth doctor had prescribed "an ounce of whiskey every evening," which had delighted his grandfather, and had caused his grandmother to wonder about the doctor's good sense.

The lichens on Katahdin had been mustard yellow, gray, brown, crusty, blazes of color on bleak boulders. Kirksey had never seen lichens in such riot before: orange, arced, sprayed from nozzled cans, wiped on the rocks with painters' rags, speckled with brown here, there green mossy rashes on yellow smears.

On the very peak had been the biggest cairn of all, and a box for messages, and the pronouncement by sign that here was the end of the Appalachian Trail, so and so many thousands of miles to Springer Mountain, Georgia. Kirksey had thought, yes, that's true. It was stuff he knew, felt close to, believing that the AT was a part of who he was, a little seen, always sensed infinite meandering, a path of stitches sewing up America and stitching him to her, to her fogbound spruce, to wet granite, snowfalls, backpacks, gas stoves, small aluminum boxes ordered from REI, grommets, efforts at home-made pemmican. Kirksey was an American, stitched to the earth by this trail, by the thousands of miles he had hiked and was yet to hike, on this trail and others, knowing peace and wonder.

When his grandfather died, it had been a fact, no real grieving. Something to be dealt with. Still, he was gone, and they wouldn't do Katahdin again.

KIRKSEY'S MOTHER
HAD A FANTASY

Kirksey's mother Jeanette was the oldest of four children. Her mother Effie called upon Jeanette to wash dishes after every meal. Jeanette did it, pretty much gladly, year after year. There was a window above the kitchen sink. Jeanette told Kirksey that she often thought about throwing the dishes out the window.

NECKS AND ASSHOLES

Kirksey's mother had for years asked for turkey dark meat, only to astonish him in her eighties by telling him that she didn't really like dark meat. It was just that she knew her children liked white meat, so she chose dark for herself. Not even her husband, Kirksey's father, had suspected this, he not being given to introspection on the possibility of kindness in others, although he had on the topic of fried chicken accused his wife of preferring "necks and assholes."

This phrase, the exact words, had often surfaced to the delight of the Kirksey and his siblings, the father at this point not being wholly intoxicated, though a sure portent of things to come, because it was so off-color. Yet Kirksey and his brothers knew their father was right. Their mother would always choose the scrawniest, least attractive chicken pieces for herself, those flawed either by anatomy or preparation, saying they were what she really wanted.

Kirksey had had a cousin who had brought her mother, then widowed, a pound of gizzards for her birthday, intending to fix them for her, only to learn that her mother disliked gizzards, had disliked them all her married years, and had only chosen the brown contortion from the platter so that her children and mate might have a wider choice.

Kirksey guessed it was a motherhood thing, not specifically Southern, although it was true the cousin's mother had been an Agnes Scott graduate, and that Kirksey's own mother had lived long enough in Georgia that she could well have learned it there.

BUTTERBALL

Kirksey had read that there had been a discussion among the Founding Fathers as to whether the wild turkey or the eagle should be the national bird. They knew the bird chosen would become our totem, our sacred object. It would be an emblem for all Americans. Benjamin Franklin had plumped for the turkey and he had lost, so the bald eagle became America's national bird, and Franklin had had to go to Paris to chase women, or peace, or something.

Still, Kirksey thought, if the turkey had won, there might have been coins with the turkey. At first it would certainly have been the tall angular wild version: bearded, wily, intelligent, friend of the Pilgrims. But with the passage of time, and the changing of the turkey itself, the coins would feature today's turkey, the Butterball. It would fit snugly on the back of a coin, a half dollar say, all trussed up and frozen, plastic protective wrap gleaming under fishnet, drumsticks poking up against the plastic, ankle bones straining to be released into the American oven.

For this coin there would be no scrabbly horned feet to render through meticulous engraving, no delicate overlapping of primary and secondary feathers, no flaring tail in strut or trailing in flight. It would be the Butterball as we know him in the freezer case. There could even be a larger coin, the silver dollar perhaps, with the family gathered round to eat the totem. Butterball atop the family table, roasted and aromatic, wisps of steam suggested by the engraver.

How different would America's politics be, her resolve and national purpose, if several times a year, Christmas and Thanksgiving at least, America ate the totem? It would set her apart from feckless nations, the French for example, who have no totem at all, or the Canadians, who have a totem they cannot eat, the state of Florida.

The Butterball of today, after a few short generations of inbreeding, has become luscious and heavy-breasted, with delicate and thoughtful segregations of white and dark meat.

Ben Franklin had simply been wrong for once in his life. The man who had flown the kite and invented eyeglasses had had to go to France, defeated, to live for years with people of no totem and very few consonants.

CROAKERS AND COURT

Kirksey's daughter had stood at the pier rail for hours, throwing out the weighted line, catching croakers and laughing, pulling them up the thirty feet of air, calling out, "I've got a big one, Daddy!" knowing it wasn't true, just happy to be catching fish. She'd hold the fish and carefully back the hook out, throw him back: "Bye, bye, Mr. Croaker. Go tell your big brother to bite my hook."

He'd taught her to put squid on the line. She would bait up and throw the line out again, the white strips waving in the air, flying from the top-and-bottom rig, two ounces of pyramidal lead pulling them down, taking the rig hard into the rolling waves and to the bottom. Twenty-pound mono, Kirksey knew it was overkill for these little fish, but then you might catch a ray or even a shark, and then what would you do, if you had six-pound test?

In thirty seconds she'd have another. She had learned to reel back in just until the line was gently taut, that was tricky, and wait hardly breathing for the tug. It took a while for her to learn to keep the line just so, not bounce the weight across the bottom. Until she got the feel for it she would think she had a fish, feeling the pull of the bouncing lead, while the fish stripped off the squid.

It was a lot like raising children, Kirksey thought. You couldn't be slack or you'd miss the clues. And you couldn't tight-line them either, not kids, or you'd bounce them, get false signals, think you'd found things that needed fixing, try to fix them, get no fish, wonder why.

Kirksey had heard the litany of failures over and over in court. The tales of parenting gone bad, glaring incidents, small failures. His docket was now mostly domestic, a welcome change from search and seizure, endless motions, suppression hearings. It's not the issues which were better in domestic court, nothing could beat the criminal law for intellectual content, it was that in family law there was the chance that he could help. He knew he did help, sorting out others' problems well enough to give their kids a chance to climb.

So, sitting in a black robe, he the putative swift and sure dispenser of perfect solutions, he knew he only had a chance at being useful if he listened carefully to the parents' words, listened carefully to the children's stumbling, embarrassed, often coached mumblings. Kirksey had a chance if he thought hard about what was really going on, if he listened for successes in school, in sports, in music lessons, and from all that maybe built a trellis for the vines to climb.

CLEAN SOCKS

Kirksey loved clean socks, especially the ragg socks his bailiff had given him for Christmas, thick warm and comfortable socks. Kirksey thought he might be turning into a boring guy, someone with no zip, but there it was: He loved taking a pair of clean ragg socks out of his suitcase when he was on a trip, say, and smell the smell of home, unroll and stretch the socks, and pull them on. What a bore.

Or was it just clean joy in simple things? The stuff Julie Andrews sang about,

Raindrops on roses and whiskers on kittens
Bright copper kettles and warm woollen mittens
Brown paper packages tied up with strings
These are a few of my favorite things

Maybe so, maybe it was clean joy, maybe all was well, maybe socks were just part of his personal list of favorite things.

GLIDERS

In the late 1940's Kirksey's grocery store got great stuff at the beginning of summer. Wax lips and teeth, big pink lips you could hold with your teeth. Big projecting teeth to slip over your incisors, smooth and soft once you warmed them up. Black wax mustaches you could hold in place by biting on a wax projection, the mustache so huge that it came down over your upper lip.

Yo-yos, sometimes even see-through yo-yos out of plastic, translucent yellow, with the string all curled up around the shaft. And tubes of colored sugar water that were whistles once you had drunk all the liquid out, well, sucked it out, there being a vacuum and you having to be careful not to collapse the wax walls by sucking too hard. All the neat stuff was out of wax, except the yo-yos of course.

And the gliders, the balsa wood gliders. They were there all year long, not seasonal. Sometimes one of the older boys would buy a folding-wing balsa glider, really expensive, the kind you launched with a rubber band sling, high high up, where at the top of the rise the wings would snap open and the plane would fly so far you might not find it sometimes, or it would land high up in a tree and you'd have to throw rocks at it to get it down. Of course, this at times would destroy the airplane.

When Kirksey got older, he realized some men did that with their love. He'd seen it far too often. Destroy love to get it back, to get the airplane down. "We had to bomb the hamlet to save it." The rock had been well intentioned, it just broke the wing off, or crushed the fuselage. And there it would be, spiraling down, gutshot, bumping into branches as it fell, ruined, angular. It wouldn't fly again, wouldn't trust again. Might get taken home to get taped up, might not. Wouldn't fly right ever again, anyway, being too heavy from the tape and out of line.

The nickel gliders were better in the long run, even though you couldn't fling them up so high. They lasted and lasted.

FOOTBALL

In high school Kirksey had played football against TSD, the Tennessee School for the Deaf. A strong team. And dirty too. Kirksey could not remember whether Webb had won or lost. He did remember that Webb had posted a four-out-of-seven season. Since that was the first year Webb had had a football team, that was pretty good.

TSD snapped the ball whenever they were ready. Kirksey didn't know how they knew when they were ready. There was no calling signals. TSD also pinched you in the pile ups. That was new.

Kirksey had played both ways, offense and defense. He had been in the line because his eyesight was bad without glasses. He could have been in the backfield as a runner, but coach had better ball carriers than Kirksey. Shuttleworth was really good, and he could catch passes. He could see them coming.

In high school Kirksey had sold Cokes at UT football games. On a good day Kirksey would make seven dollars. He carried rectangular buckets filled with ice up and down the aisles. Cokes and also 7 Ups in glass bottles. Kirksey would pull the cap off with a flourish and make it fly away. Then he would pour the drink into a cup and pass the cup down the row to the customer, who would pass money back.

Drinks cost twenty cents. Often Kirksey would be paid with a quarter which was very very good. There was some finesse in serving 7 Ups, because sometimes there would be dirt in the cup. So Kirksey would save that cup and use it for Cokes. He had been at the 1958 UT-Chattanooga game when Chattanooga defeated Tennessee. This was unheard of. Chattanooga fans stormed the field and tore down the goal posts. Police intervened massively, which prolonged what became a riot. It lasted for hours, on the field and later on Cumberland Avenue. Kirksey thought the whole thing was marvellous, he having never seen a riot before.

Kentucky games were always cold, being at the end of the season. Often there was snow. At one of them, Kirksey had thrown snowballs from his seat in Section S, Row 30 at the backs of the Kentucky players.

On November 25, 1950, Kentucky lost to Tennessee 0-7. It was the team's only loss that year. Kentucky was coached by Bear Bryant, and it was the number one team in the nation.

BEARS AND HUMMINGBIRDS

Last year Kirksey had gotten to know a mother bear and her four cubs. They became his friends, as much as it was possible for a human being to be friendly with bears. But he was always glad to see them. The cubs would wrestle, tumbling on the deck between the chairs. They would climb on the railing and walk. They would eat dogwood berries from the trees they could reach from the banister. Kirksey's deck was a playground.

When the second year arrived, the cubs came back. At least he thought these new bears were the cubs. The mother bear did not come back. The bears were interested in the hummingbird feeder. They would look at it, but they could not reach it. As the summer continued, the bears got taller and taller and were almost but not quite able to reach the feeder and pull it down.

In October no hummingbirds had been to the feeder for days, so Kirksey believed they had all migrated. His brother in upper New York state thought so too. So Kirksey took the hummingbird feeder down. The bears continued to come. They looked for the hummingbird feeder.

Earlier, Kirksey had had seed feeders for the birds. They had hung down from the eaves of the cabin far enough that a grown bear could easily reach them. When Kirksey saw he was about to lose a feeder, he would shoot the bear with his .22 pistol loaded with number 12 shot. The shot was tiny, almost dust. It did not hurt the bear, but it did alarm him. A loud noise and lots of smoke. Kirksey was careful not to shoot the bear in his face. But eventually the bears destroyed each of the seed feeders. So Kirksey stopped buying them.

SNOWFALLS

When it snowed in East Tennessee, it was a great event. It didn't happen every year that there'd be enough snow to add to the string of marvelous memories Kirksey had. As an adult Kirksey clung to snowfalls with passionate childish intensity, the same intense devotion he had had as a child.

He could remember how the power line outside his fifth-grade window had stacked up with snow, right on the wire, an ever-mounting knife-edge of snow, thin as the wire itself, one inch, then two, three, four inches, all balanced on the wire, while he and the other children had watched, awed, unbelieving, wondering when the principal would close the school, talking of being marooned, snowbound, sleeping all night under their desks. They had seen the custodian come out of the furnace room underneath the classroom, go back in, taking his shovel with him. Too much snow to even start shoveling.

They watched the kickball field get deeper and deeper, the swing set becoming eerie with snow on the ridgepole and seats. Not a breath of air, just flakes falling. It was evening all afternoon. It was snowing, and it was going to snow. When Kirksey had read those lines by Wallace Stevens years later, he thought back to that classroom, that afternoon with its gray light, the certainty of great adventure.

When he had been eight and Kirksey had still lived in Fort Sanders, there had been a big snowfall after Thanksgiving, then a melting for a few hours, enough to make water run in the alley behind the house, then a hard freeze which lasted for days. The alley behind his house had frozen solid with gray wavelets trapped in time, hard as steel. When he had pulled his sled out onto the wavelets, it clattered.

Getting on the sled was like sitting down on concrete six feet thick. He steered with his feet at first, until he was brave enough to go belly down, face skimming just inches above the surface, gravel trapped down under the ice, he could see it, sometimes it poked up through the ice and rasped on the runners, down the alley and right out onto Twentieth Street, no traffic, nobody could drive, right across Twentieth and into the next alley. Then Kirksey would go back up and do it again, his Massachusetts snowsuit bulky around his legs, a one-piece front-zipper job made by his mother on her black Singer portable. His snowsuit was fantastic equipment, like his Flexible Flyer, also from Massachusetts, a wonder of Northern technology, fast, the best in the neighborhood.

He remembered the snows back there in Boston, the bitter cold, the smell of coffee roasting in Scollay Square where his mother went shopping. The sudden warmth and smells stepping into a Fanny Farmer store for a treat. The steam issuing from manhole covers, to be whipped away by wind arcing through the canyon of streets. The light bright and cold.

He remembered his own street, Grasmere Road, filling up with snow feet deep, the known forms of steps, hydrants, and bushes turning into soft rounded mounds. Other worldly. Kirksey remembered being out alone at night, still before supper but full dark, no one about, just streetlights and falling flakes, falling gently through cones of light below the porcelained tin lamp shades.

He remembered building snow caves with the boy from behind his house one lot over, real snow houses two could get into and hunker down and think, "Well, we did it. What's next?" He remembered making snow angels by falling backward onto a bed of white, feathers flying up, flapping his arms to make wings, getting up carefully to marvel at sculptured deity. And someone's mother had made snow candy by pouring hot stuff on the snow, and it hardened and wasn't any good, but the idea had been good.

Throwing snowballs had not been important in Boston, he had been too small, or his mittens had been too puffy, lined ones, also made on the Singer portable. He wondered if there were any mothers anywhere any more who still made mittens, or did they just buy them from stores, ready made in Costa Rica or Honduras or some place where it never snowed.

For Kirksey, throwing snowballs had started in Tennessee, where it had become daring illegality, fair game those cars and trucks, panel vans, a smasher right on the oncoming windshield, chains going brack-brack-brack inside fender wells. Slush hissing away from tires, gritty sand mixed in, scattered from city garbage trucks pressed into strange service. Sedans, moving vans, maybe even a police car, well, no, but you could think about it. People shook their fists, or didn't even notice. Sudden shots from behind bushes, splashing on hoods, passenger doors, making wonderful clomps of sound, spraying explosions of white skidding up and over windows and roofs.

Once Kirksey hit a car with three boys, UT students maybe, and they chased him. He ran behind the line of houses, downhill into the woods, tripping and falling. He lay still, hoping he wouldn't be found, but they found him. He tried being unconscious, knocked out, then he acted groggy and hurt, and the boys relented and told him to be careful and not do that no more, shit, what did he think, poor little kid.

HUNGARY AND LATIN

After college, Kirksey spent a year in Austria studying German literature to get ready for graduate school. His German became so good he could pass for a native of Styria, Austria's Steiermark. In the spring of 1965, he took a short bus ride to Budapest.

After three hours in Budapest, he was disoriented, unhappy. The landscape was not different from Austria, and Budapest was a big city like Vienna. Kirksey walked the streets feeling worse and worse. He went from one place to another, using his guidebook. He took some pictures from the hill, drank a glass of tea. Even the tea failed to lift his mood.

At the summit of the hill was St. Stephen's cathedral. The guidebook said he should go. Kirksey didn't care. He felt rootless, lost. He wanted to check out of his hotel, walk to the bus station, and get back to Austria. What was it about Hungary? Was he getting sick? He hadn't eaten anything strange, none of those sausages with names he didn't recognize. He had eaten a roll, played it safe. Kirksey felt lost inside an Ingmar Bergman film without words.

He pushed his way into the cathedral, dropped a few coins in the collection box, and gazed at the stained glass windows. He felt better at once. There were words there he could read. Latin, wonderful Latin. It was in the windows, on the grave markers, at the stations of the cross. Kirksey felt his miasma lift. He could read again. He had the written word back, the Western tradition, he knew where he was. No more impossible Ugric lump words, not a cognate anywhere, the simplest everyday vocabulary beyond his grasp. He loved this church, its architecture. He liked Hungary fine. He was glad he had come.

TWO THINGS MADE KIRKSEY WHO HE WAS

Kirksey knew that there were two things which had done the most to make him who he was: tackle football and the Boy Scouts. When he said this to others they were surprised. They asked, "Well, what about living in Austria and Berlin? What about that PhD? What about law school?" Kirksey would say that those things were important, but only as add-ons to the foundation of football and scouting.

Football had taught Kirksey about exhaustion, and that he could keep going even when exhausted. That he disliked heat, disliked sweat running into his eyes, and disliked having his finger dislocated. He saw a friend's leg broken, another friend's knee dislocated.

He learned that there was a rock sticking out of the thirty-five yard line in Coalfield, Tennessee, and that beating Coalfield on their home field meant your bus would be vandalized and you'd be late getting back to Knoxville.

When Kirksey talked about the Boy Scouts, it raised the eyebrows of people who knew about sexual scandals. Kirksey was sorry about the scandals and the cloud it had cast. He supposed there were similarities with the Catholic Church, the code of silence and all that. It was a shame for both institutions, Kirksey thought. He told himself an acid bath of publicity was a good thing maybe, even though it hurt him personally for the Boy Scouts.

Football had been combat, endurance, suffering, and sometimes victory. Sometimes it was a defeat in the score, but it was never a defeating activity. It remained valid. One of Kirksey's own sons had played football. Kirksey was glad of that. Kirksey knew there were parents who kept their sons out of football for fear of injury, especially mental injury. He understood that.

KIRKSEY'S PURSUIT
OF PERFECTION

For Kirksey pursuit of perfection brought peace. He knew that pursuit had figured in America's founding documents as the pursuit of happiness. For Kirksey the pursuit of happiness was doing well what he was good at.

To write well was important to Kirksey. Cogent self-expression, thoughts well-formed, well sequenced, explaining what was on his mind. Also gardening. The layout, the appearance, the maturation of the vegetables--all of this was satisfying. When done well, it was more than gratifying; it was uplifting.

Studying birds. He did it well, systematically, with tabs in fifteen books--some of the books in Knoxville, some in Gatlinburg. He marked his recurring species. He was also getting good at identifying bird calls, even better now that he had hearing aids. This was a real joy. It was another example of perfection pursued.

Kirksey's faith life was a pursuit of perfection. He knew that in an area such as religious faith perfection did not exist, because the scope of the search was as infinite as God. But the pursuit was there and was joyous.

THOUGHTS

A FRIEND TEACHES YOU TO FISH

A person doesn't have many close friends. But if you have one who teaches you to fish, he is a true friend. He is a friend who never knows where his influence stops. Henry Adams said about teaching, "A teacher affects eternity. He never knows where his influence stops."

It is that way with friendship. A friend benefits his friend and that friend passes it on to others downstream.

My friend taught me to fish. I taught my brother to fish. My brother is now a better fisherman than I am. I taught my wife to fish. She is not better at fishing than I am, but she is luckier. I taught my daughter to fish. She absolutely loves it. She is not better than I am, but that is not the point, the point is her enjoyment. And now he is teaching her own son to fish. I taught my two sons to fish. One of them taught his three sons to fish. And all this came from that first friend who taught me to fish. He did it never knowing that he was affecting eternity.

WRITE NOW!

A lot of people are afraid to write. They feel diffident, not quite up to it, not adequate to the task. And so they don't try. This is fear of failure, it is approach-avoidance. But simply put, all of us can speak and think, and that is all you need in order to write. Because we can all articulate our thoughts orally, there is no bar to articulating them on paper, except our own fear. The critical thing is to begin.

There's no writing "tomorrow." Tomorrow just means "someday" or "when I get around to it." But I say, "Write now!" Don't correct and polish as you go. Just get out a first draft, or just write the start of whatever it is you are thinking about. It doesn't matter if it has typos, is graceless, or embarrasses you. One easy way to get a first draft, warts and all, is to use voice typing. Most PCs come with it now.

The point is, that horrible first draft is a beginning. You can edit it later. The most important thing is to get it down once. In any old form.

Stick with what you are good at. Not even my wife likes my fiction. So I stick with what I am good at, nonfiction on topics I know about. There are things which you know better than anyone else in the world. More intensely, with more feeling. It doesn't matter whether those things are things for fiction or nonfiction. You are the expert. More than that, you are the best person in the world to get those things in front of other people. Pat yourself on the back. You are the big cheese. The only cheese who can do it.

COWPIES

To step in a cowpie is to commit an unforced error. You look all around a pasture field for something stupid to do and, seeing a cow pie in the corner of the field, you rush to it and step in the middle. It happens.

Cocke County Child Support Magistrate Lu Ann Hatcher Bellew did just that in 2013. She decided that a man and woman who were before her in a child support case could not, should not, must not name their baby "Messiah."

Ballew got national headlines for opining that "Messiah" is a name reserved for Jesus Christ. She ordered that the name be stricken from the eight-month-old baby's birth certificate. The boy's parents, Jalessa Martin and Jawaan McCullough, had not asked that Messiah's first name be changed. They only wanted to change the baby's last name to "McCullough" to reflect Jawaan McCullough's legal status as the baby's father.

In her ruling, Ballew wrote: "Messiah means Savior, Deliverer, the One who will restore God's Kingdom. Messiah is a title that is held only by Jesus Christ." She also opined the name Messiah might subject the boy to harassment by Christians in Cocke County.

Fortunately, the Cocke County mess got fixed. Fourth Judicial District Chancellor Telford Forgety overturned Bellew's decision. He ruled that Ballew had violated the establishment clause of the U.S. Constitution, prohibiting the governmental endorsement of a particular religion.

COPPERHEADS

The moral equivalent of a copperhead snake is the lawyer who tried to bug my home. He told a private investigator who was an expert in electronic surveillance that he needed to "get something" on Judge Swann. Happily, the P.I. turned down the job and came to me. The attorney had said he needed "an edge, just something."

Had that not been the case--had the lawyer in fact learned some interesting detail with which to bring pressure on me, what would I have done? Cave in? Do his bidding? Go public with the attempt? Seek criminal redress whatever the embarrassment might be?

Ask yourself how many persons being blackmailed find it better to pay the blackmailer. Imagine the consequences for justice if a judge is compromised by blackmail. The entire courthouse slides into the river.

SEE SEVEN STATES FROM ROCK CITY

"See seven states from Rock City," shout barns and road signs throughout Tennessee. Well maybe.

When you are at Rock City above the city of Chattanooga, you can certainly look toward your feet and see a piece of Tennessee. Or move a little and look at your feet and see Alabama or Georgia, since Lookout Mountain is in all three states.

At Rock City's elevation of 2392 feet, you are also supposed to be able to see four more states: Mississippi, Kentucky, North Carolina, and South Carolina. As I say, maybe. They are not painted different colors as they are in puzzles or maps of the United States. Too bad. Then we would know.

Rock City is completely natural, made by God. Dollywood is completely unnatural, made by Dolly. They are both good places to visit, and completely different. Rock City is less expensive than Dollywood.

All in all, if you can only go to one, go to Rock City. From which you can see seven States.

Or not.

A POEM FOR DIANA, ABOUT SAINTS

Saint Valentine, I call upon you,
For you are the patron saint of beekeepers.
Diana and I are beekeepers. Or we were once.
But, I guess, once a beekeeper, always a beekeeper.
Valentine, help me write this poem for Diana.
She's my wife, my blessed wife, of twenty-three years.
That stretch of time is the blink of an eye--
An eternity of endless joy,
Twenty-three Christmases, twenty-three Epiphanies,
Forty-six birthdays.

You started it all, Valentine, this sending of cards.
And then you died.
Well, no, then you were beheaded.
I hope that doesn't happen to me.
But if it does, I can start a class action against Hallmark.
I mean, you knew this stuff was risky, Valentine,
This falling-in-love stuff and sending out cards.
Well, no, my estate can file the class action.
So, Diana, administratrix, you should keep that in mind.

Saint Patrick did not drive the snakes out of Ireland.
But he could have. Yup.
Would'a, could'a, should'a.
(If they'd'a been there.)
But they weren't. Nope. No snakes to drive out.
Too bad.
It was something about there being no land bridge
For the little wigglies to cross over from England.
Oh, well.
But still, Saint Patrick gets the credit.
He has good PR.
He has a church in New York with green candles.

Saint Valentine doesn't need any extra PR.
He's his own department of public relations.
No employees. He just cranks out cards using contract labor.
He has card racks that stretch for yards and yards
At Kroger, Walgreens, Food City.
Hey, probably in hardware stores too.
Yards and yards of public relations
For the patron saint of love.

Saint Francis is local. He stands in our gardens,
Humble, loving, holding a bird. Another bird sits on his shoulder.
He's with us twice at our house--in front,
And also in the raised beds.
Because, well, that's as it should be.
We need him with us twice,
So that we remember his busy life--
Founding the order, his devotion to the poor,
His devotion to all the animals,
His trip to Egypt, his persuasion of the wolf.
He didn't stop there. He founded the Poor Clares,

He made the first Christmas créche.
A regular workaholic. No need for PR.
He preached to the birds. He called them his sisters.
I wonder if he preaches to our chickens.

Saint Anthony finds things.
Now, there's another saint who gets things done.
Not a workaholic like Francis, but always ready to help.
He has a lot of work to do. I mean a lot, just for us.
My glasses, sometimes my truck keys.
Sometimes Diana's smartphone,
Which isn't so smart, because it keeps losing itself.
Saint Anthony doesn't need PR.
He's Martha Stewart absent profit motive.
He's good to have around, easy to listen to, like Martha.
Gives good advice, like Martha, helps us live better.
Anthony works and works, never gets paid,
Except in thanks, the best payment.
Martha gets paid 'cause we buy her stuff.
We have a whole room of her stuff.
It's in the basement.

So this is my valentine for you, my Diana,
My dear one, my blink-of-the eye Diana.
It's light-hearted, this valentine, unique, a lot of fun.
It's like our marriage.
You can forget about snakes and Ireland
And poor old Saint Patrick having no work to do.
Well, no snake work.
And you can forget Saint Francis for now. He's doing fine.
You can forget Saint Anthony too, for now.
Just concentrate today on Saint Valentine.
Unless of course--can't rule it out--
Saint Anthony helped us find each other.

Which, if he did, it would be
Sort of a Valentine/Anthony teamwork thing.
You know, a dynamic duo, a Marvel team,
Coming soon to a theatre near you.
Without snakes.

--Valentine's Day, 2020

LOVE, CHRIST, AND THE EVERLY BROTHERS

Christ walked the walk of love. He did it by example and by kindness. He astounded by his miracles, but he led by his kindness. He led the ever-bumbling Peter, he led the woman at the well, he led his disciples by washing their feet, he praised the woman who wet his hair with her tears, healed the woman who touched his robe, healed the centurion's sick servant because the centurion had deep faith, praised the widow who gave her mite, touched and healed lepers.

Love is commitment, devotion, head-over-heels enlistment. It says, "I am yours. You are mine. We are together. We will be in heaven together even if we should get there apart." Our children watch and wonder, "Can we do this too?"

Felice and Boudleaux Bryant put it this way for the Everly Brothers in 1958:

Darling you can count on me
'Til the sun dries up the sea
Until then I'll always be
Devoted to you

Judge Bill Swann

I'll be yours through endless time
I'll adore your charms sublime
Guess by now you'll know that I'm
Devoted to you

I'll never hurt you
I'll never lie
I'll never be untrue
I'll never give you reason to cry
I'd be unhappy
If you were blue

Through the years our love will grow
Like a river it will flow
It can't die because I'm so
Devoted to you

And Goethe treated love this way in 1774:
Es war ein König in Thule,
Gar treu bis an das Grab,
Dem sterbend seine Buhle
Einen goldnen Becher gab.

Es ging ihm nichts darüber,
Er leert' ihn jeden Schmaus;
Die Augen gingen ihm über,
So oft er trank daraus.

Love is devotion. It is undying. It will last. It will be there when someone sings one last song for me.

KATHY

I like to say I have three doctorates--a Yale PhD (German Literature), my beloved JD from the University of Tennessee George C. Taylor School of Law, and a third doctorate in Elected Office Politics (EOP).

After four campaigns for those eight-year terms, my EOP degree comprises more intense learning than my formal trainings ever did. And one of those campaigns gave me a fourth wife, and possibly even more than four. (An election opponent, David Lee, accused me of concealing various divorces from multiple wives, one of whom was definitively stated to be "Kathy", a nurse.

I have searched throughout Tennessee for Kathy and been unable to find her, but she lives on happily in Swann family mythology. "Kathy" is responsible for many of my omissions and errors. Indeed, if you don't have a Kathy in your home life, you probably should invent one.

SHAKESPEARE'S HENRY

Even kings can improve. Shakespeare's *Henry V* follows his two plays which dealt with young prince Hal: *Henry IV Part 1*, *Henry IV Part 2*. Prince Hal ascended the throne in 1413 becoming Henry V, and died nine years later in 1422, at the age of 35.

Shakespeare is at pains to present the House of Lancaster favorably. We see Prince Hal in ribaldry, growing into the role and responsibility of a king.

But with the presentation of the new king on his French campaign, Shakespeare takes a significant risk: He shows us a king engaged in on-the-job training. And not doing a very good job.

There are two speeches, one bad and one good, delivered to the troops. Here is what I believe is a bad one:

Once more unto the breach, dear friends, once more;
Or close the wall up with our English dead.
In peace there's nothing so becomes a man
As modest stillness and humility:
But when the blast of war blows in our ears,
Then imitate the action of the tiger;
Stiffen the sinews, summon up the blood,
Disguise fair nature with hard-favour'd rage;

Then lend the eye a terrible aspect;
Let pry through the portage of the head
Like the brass cannon; let the brow o'erwhelm it
As fearfully as doth a galled rock
O'erhang and jutty his confounded base,
Swill'd with the wild and wasteful ocean.
Now set the teeth and stretch the nostril wide,
Hold hard the breath and bend up every spirit
To his full height. On, on, you noblest English.
Whose blood is fet from fathers of war-proof!
Fathers that, like so many Alexanders,
Have in these parts from morn till even fought
And sheathed their swords for lack of argument:
Dishonour not your mothers; now attest
That those whom you call'd fathers did beget you.
Be copy now to men of grosser blood,
And teach them how to war. And you, good yeoman,
Whose limbs were made in England, show us here
The mettle of your pasture; let us swear
That you are worth your breeding; which I doubt not;
For there is none of you so mean and base,
That hath not noble lustre in your eyes.
I see you stand like greyhounds in the slips,
Straining upon the start. The game's afoot:
Follow your spirit, and upon this charge
Cry 'God for Harry, England, and Saint George!'
--Act III, Scene i, the siege of Harfleur

Since this is a famous speech, you are surprised that I call it a bad one. But imagine yourself among the foot soldiers before the walls of Harfleur fortress, September 1415. There is a breach in the wall from earlier English efforts, and we foot soldiers may be on the verge of victory. We are tired.

We are far from home. We may die. We have a young king. We hope he has something inspiring to tell us.

Once more unto the breach, dear friends, once more;
Or close the wall up with our English dead.

Our king is talking to us about our deaths, our bodies stacked in the breach. He would do better to tell us about victory and glory and booty. But no, he tells us to get our game face on:

In peace there's nothing so becomes a man
As modest stillness and humility:
But when the blast of war blows in our ears,
Then imitate the action of the tiger;
Stiffen the sinews, summon up the blood,
Disguise fair nature with hard-favour'd rage;

This was a golden opportunity for the young king to speak sincere words of encouragement. Instead, he launched into an elaborate essay about body parts--eyes, eye sockets, brows, teeth, and nostrils.

Then lend the eye a terrible aspect;
Let pry through the portage of the head
Like the brass cannon; let the brow o'erwhelm it
As fearfully as doth a galled rock
O'erhang an
d jutty his confounded base,
Swill'd with the wild and wasteful ocean.
Now set the teeth and stretch the nostril wide,

Let's see now, say the footsoldiers, I've got to let my eye stick out like a cannon, but with my forehead hanging over it like a cliff rock at the ocean. I can do the part with the teeth and nostrils. What silly thing will he say next?

Hold hard the breath and bend up every spirit
To his full height. On, on, you noblest English.

Well, that's better say the footsoldiers. He's going to launch into a speech of encouragement.

Whose blood is fet from fathers of war-proof!
Fathers that, like so many Alexanders,
Have in these parts from morn till even fought
And sheathed their swords for lack of argument:

No, we were wrong, say the footsoldiers. The king is off on another tangent. Who is this Alexander guy? Did the king know my father? How come the argument stopped? Oh, say the footsoldiers, we get it. All the enemies are dead, so the argument is over. Well, all right then, they think. What's he going to say next?

Dishonour not your mothers; now attest
That those whom you call'd fathers did beget you.

My mother? Why talk about our mothers? Is he suggesting we are bastards?

Be copy now to men of grosser blood,
And teach them how to war.

OK, who are these soldiers of grosser blood we are supposed to teach? Is he talking about the enemy? I hope not. We are supposed to help the enemy fight better?

And you, good yeoman,
Whose limbs were made in England, show us here
The mettle of your pasture; let us swear
That you are worth your breeding; which I doubt not;
For there is none of you so mean and base,
That hath not noble lustre in your eyes.

So, we are mean and base, but he doubts not our breeding because our eyes are noble? Probably because they stick out like cannons over the ocean?

I see you stand like greyhounds in the slips,
Straining upon the start. The game's afoot:
Follow your spirit, and upon this charge
Cry 'God for Harry, England, and Saint George!'

Well, say the footsoldiers, at least he gives us a good send-off.

I have taken terrible liberties with Henry's speech. At every opportunity for cavilling, I do so. At every opportunity for misunderstanding, I do so. But I say Henry's speech is not effective rhetoric, not effective communication. It is a bombastic collection of images which would have been lost on a common soldier. The speech could have been so much better.

But I think that this is exactly Shakespeare's point. Henry is going to improve. At the end of the campaign, a month later at the battle of Agincourt, 25 October 1415, St. Crispin's Day, he addresses his troops lovingly, masterfully:

Rather proclaim it, Westmoreland, through my host,
That he which hath no stomach to this fight,
Let him depart; his passport shall be made,

And crowns for convoy put into his purse;
We would not die in that man's company
That fears his fellowship to die with us.
This day is call'd the feast of Crispian.
He that outlives this day, and comes safe home,
Will stand a tip-toe when this day is nam'd,
And rouse him at the name of Crispian.
He that shall live this day, and see old age,
Will yearly on the vigil feast his neighbours,
And say "To-morrow is Saint Crispian."
Then will he strip his sleeve and show his scars,
And say "These wounds I had on Crispin's day."
Old men forget; yet all shall be forgot,
But he'll remember, with advantages,
What feats he did that day. Then shall our names,
Familiar in his mouth as household words-
Harry the King, Bedford and Exeter,
Warwick and Talbot, Salisbury and Gloucester-
Be in their flowing cups freshly rememb'red.
This story shall the good man teach his son;
And Crispin Crispian shall ne'er go by,
From this day to the ending of the world,
But we in it shall be remembered-
We few, we happy few, we band of brothers;
For he today that sheds his blood with me
Shall be my brother; be he ne'er so vile,
This day shall gentle his condition;
And gentlemen in England now-a-bed
Shall think themselves accurs'd they were not here,
And hold their manhoods cheap whiles any speaks
That fought with us upon Saint Crispin's day.
--Act IV, Scene iii, the Saint Crispin's Day speech

This is a declaration of brotherly love, a proud request for shared suffering. I will die in your company gladly, if you will fight with me. We will be forever remembered for what we do here today. We will stand tall on every Saint Crispin's Day, my brothers.

Henry is now ready to be king.

SPEAKING LOCAL

In East Tennessee we say "poke sallet" for polk salad; "I come home yestiddy"; and "I done done it."

"You'uns" is the local downgrade of the southern "you all." As in, "You'uns ain't got a lick a sense."

"I don't care to" means both, "No, thanks, I don't want to do it," and its exact opposite, "Sure, I'll do it."

"Hit don't make no never mind," means "It doesn't matter." Logically the negatives would mean it does matter. But the double/triple negative does not operate.

"Hit's kindly bright in here," means it is too bright in here. "Kindly" means "kind of." It is used in complaints.

"When I'm driving alone, you don't want to be with me," is actually said in East Tennessee. A true Yogi Berra-ism.

"I reckon as how" means, "The way I figure it . . ."

"Tetched in the head," means not quite right upstairs.

"If I had my druthers" means "I would prefer to . . ." The phrase is strictly American, and not limited to East Tennessee. But we say it often.

"I got nary applesauce" means, "I don't have any applesauce." This evolved from "nary a," as in "nary a care." But in East Tennessee "nary" is a stand-alone adjective.

"They ain't give us none," means, "They didn't give us any." Once again, the double negative is not operative.

"If they's money in it" is our equivalent of "if it is worthwhile". In centuries past, the English spoke about a card game being worth the expense of burning a valuable candle.

"With my teeth in my mouth" is a way of describing inaction. "I should have done something, but I sat there with my teeth in my mouth." "Don't just stand there with your teeth in your mouth."

"Cold beer" is pronounced as one word, accenting the first syllable: "Please bring me a **cold**beer."

"Extra" is pronounced "extry." "Wheelbarrow" is often "wheelberry."

"Don't let the screen door hit ya on the way out," means, "It is time for you to leave now."

"Didn't used to could": unable to do a thing in the past. "I can do it now, but I didn't use to could." "He can ride his bike now, but he didn't use to could."

"Do you feel me?" means, "Do you know what I am saying? Do you understand me?" It is a phrase which in East Tennessee may be limited to black speakers.

"I'll swan" is said in East Tennessee, but the phrase is not limited to East Tennessee. It is widespread in America. The Oxford English Dictionary lists "swan" as a verb, labeled U.S. slang, derived, says the OED, probably from northern England dialectal "Is' wan," meaning "I shall warrant," or "I'll be bound." The OED suggests the phrase became a mincing substitute for "swear." The first use in print recorded in the dictionary is from Missouri in the year 1823.

"Not much punkin" means "not much good." "Punkin" is slang for pumpkin.

"I'll do it even if it harelips the pope" is said in East Tennessee, but it is widespread in America.

"She was sumpin" is high praise of a female. "Really something" to look at, presumably.

"Tallywacker" is widely used locally and throughout the South. It simply is another word for "penis," but avoids the perhaps embarrassing and correct biological term.

"You've got yourself a sitch-ee-aishin," means, "You've got your hands full. What are you going to do now?"

Something really difficult to do is "harder than putting socks on a rooster."

"Leakin' water like a sieve," means that the undertaking is hopeless.

EVOLVING LANGUAGE

Language continually evolves everywhere. We would all still be speaking Latin now, if language were not a constantly evolving and changing ocean of sound.

"Text" was never, ever, ever a verb. That is, until the 21st century.

Until the 21st century "impact" was always a noun. For language purists, "text" and "impact" will always be nouns and will never be verbs, but purists are being swept away by an ever-present tide of linguistic creativity.

"Unique" means "one of a kind." That's all it means. All it can mean. But tell that to the advertising industry, where every day you are offered the most unique whatever.

The very same tide which made "text" and "impact" into verbs made Latin into a new language, in fact, several new languages. The purists of the fourth century were probably upset that their beloved Latin was evolving out from under them. But, too bad, they lost.

Now we have Italian, and Spanish, and French, and Romanian, and Portuguese, and English. And no Latin at all, except snippets in the practice of law, and of church Latin, which is effectively museum Latin.

Purists are also probably losing the battle of the possessive singular. Purists know that the possessive singular is always formed by adding an apostrophe plus an "s": The fish's belly. Gilbert's pencil. Charles's friend.

The only exception is "its," which does in fact mean "possessed by the it." As in, "Its handle is broken."

"It's" is a contraction for, and means, "it is." As in, "It's too bad its handle is broken."

A HARVARD DREAM

Harvard again. I have arrived late. It is freshman year. My roommates and others I meet already have counselors who plan their course loads, sign them up for courses, get them oriented to begin college.

Not me. I have just gotten there. I have no counselor, no course load. I wander around bereft. I have no courses, and do not know where to go to get signed up. I think you sign up in University Hall, but I cannot find University Hall. On waking, it seems to have been an all night dream. The stink of perdition fills my head.

Diana asks, "Did you sleep well?"

I say, "No. I had more dreams."

"Well, were you worrying about going to court today?"

"No," I say, "it's not that. Today I am working for someone who has no money, who has been steamrolled by his wife's counsel. A lawyer who has defiled the practice of law."

In my waking hours I am a good guy. Pro bono representation, pro bono advice, pro bono counseling, pro bono hand-holding. Christian service. But I don't dream about that. I don't dream about Germany or Austria, where I was really and truly over my head at times, and from which I could have a rich harvest of crappy dreams. No. I dream of being two days behind my roommates at college.

I do not know why I should dream about being lost in an academic setting. I was never ever lost in any academic setting, except Harvard's freshman math. But being unable to do freshman math did not upset me then, and does not upset me now. But the Harvard out-of-step dream, unable to get to courses, is profoundly worrying, and each time I dream it, the situation is hopeless.

ANOTHER BAD DREAM

The Tennessee River begins upstream from Knoxville with the joining of the Holston and French Broad rivers. This is a fact. There is a street in Knoxville, Tennessee, which runs north and south named Gay Street. This is also a fact. Gay Street runs from the river and courthouse at the south end of the street straight north out of town. This is the last fact. All else is a dream.

The dream begins positively. I am not a judge. I am a lawyer again, trying cases. I have just completed a half day of trial. I have done well. There is more trial to come later that day, or the next day. It is not clear in the dream when the trial is to continue. I am walking north on Gay Street, away from the courthouse. I am on the Tennessee Theatre side of the street, about a block or two shy of the movie theatre. Here I am met and greeted by lawyers. The lawyers know of my morning success. They compliment me. I am pleased.

Then I know it is time for me to go back to where I came from, back toward the courthouse, so I turn around and head south on Gay Street. The landscape changes. It opens up diagonally to the left, and slants downward out of sight. I know this is impossible, but still I walk downhill into the slant. "This is not going to end well," I tell myself.

I do not recognize what I see, but I keep going, knowing I am lost. I will need a door key when I get there, wherever 'there' is, but I cannot find the key. It is not in my pocket. I don't remember losing it. Nor do I remember ever having had it. Not having the key produces deep dread. I am lost, and know even if I get to that door, I will not be able to open it. At this point I realize I am in a dream and make myself wake up.

In earlier years dealing with bad dreams, I considered the possibility that they were produced by the enemy, the devil. I cannot even now dismiss that as a possibility. We know in Christian theology that the devil, the enemy, the father of lies, prowls around like a lion, looking for someone to devour. That is frighteningly clear in 1 Peter 5:8. The father of lies does not want us to present ourselves to God holy and blameless as his servant. Anything to interrupt that relationship is worth it. Deep dread will interrupt that relationship.

C.S. Lewis deals with the importance of interrupting the relationship with God in his *Screwtape Letters*. He tells us that Screwtape is the most senior devil in hell. He tells us that Wormwood is a very minor devil and also Screwtape's nephew. Uncle Screwtape explains to Wormwood that all earthlings are "patients" for the devils to operate upon. Screwtape does not tell Wormwood that introducing deep dread into the patient can interfere with the patient's closeness to God. Screwtape misses a real opportunity here.

If these dreams are to continue for me, how am I to deal with them? I know that I made myself vulnerable back in high school. I told Sam Colville then that we should not rest on our laurels, but focus on the next challenge. I meant it. What comes next, I said, is what really counts. Press on. I lived that way for decades.

However, all is not bleak. I take great joy in moments of beauty. I stand and stare at autumn leaves, at flowers, at clouds, at my vegetable gardens, at Diana's flowers. These are blessed moments. They are the moments in Toby Keith's video with Clint Eastwood, "Don't Let the Old Man In."

I am a mix, I am a jumble of countervailing impulses. Perhaps all people are like this. I hope not. I would gladly live in the boredom of one hundred percent positive thoughts.

A GOOD DREAM

This dream has no facts. It is one hundred percent divorced from reality. In this dream I fly. I float in the air just high enough to be comfortable. I go from one place to another slowly. I do not fly up to 5000 feet, as in a hot air balloon. I just coast along above the ground ten or twelve feet in the air where it is interesting.

This does attract attention. People are alarmed. I tell them it is really nothing special, just an ability that I have. I say I have been favored with this ability. It has been given to me. I tell them that I'm a Christian and perhaps it was given to me by the Lord, but that I do not know that that is definitely so. But that it seems probable to me.

People tell me, "You can make money out of this, you can train other people to do it." I tell them I don't believe that is possible. I tell them that it seems to me you either have the gift or you don't. I tell them, "I suppose you could pray for it." I tell them that I did not pray for it, that it just appeared.

I tell them I enjoy it and wish that they also could fly. I tell them that they should not be alarmed or concerned. I tell them that they should simply accept this flying thing as one of God's beauties like the flowers or the autumn Leaves. "It is odd," I say, "but you will come to deal with it in time, as I have."

SONGS ABOUT WOMEN

Men's songs about women are often about jealousy, adultery, fear of loss, and loneliness. Sometimes they are about joy, exuberant joy. Women's songs about men deal with the same themes. Think of Dolly Parton's "Jolene," in which Dolly plumbs the fear of loss.

Albert Collins knows that his wife is cheating on him. He goes to work during the day and she has a party with someone in their house while he's gone. Collins comes home and finds the mess. He complains. He complains at length. He cleans up the mess, and in the spoken section of the song does some great guitar work improvising the sounds of cleaning the dirty dishes.

His woman is spending money on fancy food she never gives him. That really irks him, along with the mess.

<u>Too Many Dirty Dishes, Albert Collins</u>

Too many dirty dishes in the sink for just us two
I said, too many dirty dishes in the sink for just us two
You got me wonderin' baby
Who's makin' dirty dishes with you?

I get up an' go to work in the mo'nin'
I come right home at night
When I leave the sink is empty
When I come back home
She got 'em stacked up out of sight

Too many dirty dishes in the sink just for us two
Well you got me wonderin' baby,
Who's makin' dirty dishes with you?

(Spoken:)
Look at this kitchen!
Pots an' pans, ev'rywhere, it's pitiful!
Look at all these glasses layin' all up on the sink!
Looks like she even had a party up in here, too
You wait 'til I see this woman, when she get home
That glass over there, got a cigar in it or sump'in
I don't smoke no cigar
Um, servin' caviar
I don't eat no caviar
What's wrong with this woman?
All these pots in here, gonna run me some water right here
Yeah now, you wait 'til I see this woman when she get home
Pots 'n pans all stacked up here
There's a pot, let me scrape this pot out
Oh it's pitiful an' I don't know why this woman come an'
have a party
When I'm at work
Gettin' all this stuff under my fingernails,
Run some more water in here
Yeah, now I can wash these glasses out, wash them up first
Yeah, that's pretty clean now, though
Now I got all this, now I gotta work on these pots a little
bit more

Makes me so mad, I don't know what to do
Thought I was her husband, 'stead a maid!
Like ol red chili or somethin' all done got dried up on all these pots
She never fix me none of this good food!
You wait 'til that woman get home, I'm scrapin' all these pots for her

(Sings:)
I've done your dirty dishes
How much am I suppose to take?
When I left I had corn flakes for breakfast
Now there's a bone from a T-bone steak

Too many dirty dishes in the sink for just us two
You've got me wonderin' baby
Who in the hell is makin' dirty dishes with you?

So the cuckolded Albert Collins eats his spartan corn flakes while his woman lives high on the hog.

In "Long Tall Sally," Little Richard sings about the fun he anticipates "tonight," even while he catches Uncle John engaged in adultery. Uncle John is married to Aunt Mary, but Uncle John is pursuing Long Tall Sally, who is "built for speed" (with all the ambiguities that carries). And Uncle John has a lot of fun.

Long Tall Sally, Little Richard

I'm gonna tell Aunt Mary 'bout Uncle John
He claims he has the misery, but he has a lot of fun

Oh baby, yes, baby
Ooh baby, havin' me some fun tonight, yeah

Well, long tall Sally, she's built for speed
She got everything that Uncle John need
Oh baby, yes, baby
Ooh baby, havin' me some fun tonight, yeah

Well, I saw Uncle John with bald head Sally
He saw Aunt Mary comin' and he ducked back in the alley
Oh baby, yes, baby
Ooh baby, havin' me some fun tonight, yeah

Ooh, Have some fun tonight
Every thing's all right
Have some fun
Have me some fun tonight

Little Richard approves of what Uncle John is doing. Uncle John is having fun, and Little Richard is also going to have fun tonight.

In another Little Richard song, his "Good Golly, Miss Molly," Little Richard is pursuing Molly. He likes that she sure "likes to ball." An intentional ambiguity. He's going to buy her a diamond ring, she is going to kiss him, and then do the ambiguous "ting-a-ling-a-ling" to him.

He is really looking forward to it. We even have the Uncle John theme coming up again, adultery, when he speaks of the "mommas" that Papa has. Good themes repeat themselves in music, as in literature.

Good Golly, Miss Molly, Little Richard

Good golly, Miss Molly, sure like to ball
Good golly, Miss Molly, sure like to ball
You're rockin' and a-rollin', can't hear your momma call
From the early, early mornin' 'til the early, early night
When I caught Miss Molly rockin' at the house of blue light
Good golly, Miss Molly, sure like to ball
Oh when you're rockin' and a-rollin', you can't hear your momma call

Momma, poppa told me, "Son, you better watch your step"
If I knew poppa's mommas, have to watch my poppa self
Good golly, Miss Molly, sure like to ball
When you're rockin' and a-rollin', can't hear your momma call
Good golly Miss Molly, sure like to ball
Good golly, Miss Molly, sure like to ball.
When you're rockin' and a-rollin', can't hear your momma call

I am going to the corner, gonna buy a diamond ring
Would you pardon me, kiss me, ting-a-ling-a-ling?
Good golly, Miss Molly, sure like to ball
Oh when you're rockin' and a-rollin', can't hear your momma call

"Can't hear your mama call" echoes the Everly Brothers' "Wake Up, Little Susie" in which the singer and Susie have slept through the parental curfew.

And then in "Tutti Frutti," Little Richard blasts off into space in a paroxysm of joy, because Sue and Daisy just drive him crazy.

Tutti Frutti, Little Richard

Wop bop a loo bop a lop boom boom!
Tutti frutti, oh rutti,
Tutti frutti, oh rutti,
Tutti frutti, oh rutti,
Tutti frutti, oh rutti,
Tutti frutti, oh rutti,
Wop bop a loo mop a lop bam boom!

I got a girl named Sue, she knows just what to do,
I got a girl named Sue, she knows just what to do,
She rock to the East, she rock to the West,
But she's the girl that I love best,

Tutti frutti, oh rutti,
Tutti frutti, oh rutti, ooo
Tutti frutti, oh rutti,
Tutti frutti, oh rutti,
Tutti frutti, oh rutti,
Wop bop a loo mop a lop bam boom!

I got a girl named Daisy, she almost drives me crazy,
Got a girl named Daisy, she almost drives me crazy,
She knows how to love me, yes indeed,
Boy you don't know what she do to me,

Tutti frutti, oh rutti,
Tutti frutti, oh rutti,
Tutti frutti, oh rutti,
Wop bop a loo mop a lop bam boom!

We are adrift again in marvelous ambiguities. "Rocking" to the east, "rocking" to the west. She knows "just what to do." "Boy, you don't know what she do to me." This is more of the "ting-a-ling-a-ling."

The theme of loneliness is nowhere better expressed then in Neil Young's "A Man Needs a Maid." Not only is Young lonely, he is cut off from life. There is no one he can trust. He objectifies a woman he can purchase to do work for him. Not sexual work, but housework. All this while lacking real love because, as he says, he doesn't feel "part of." He moans, "When will I see you again?" There is a real love, and he has lost it.

A Man Needs a Maid, Neil Young

My life is changing in so many ways
I don't know who to trust anymore
There's a shadow running through my days
Like a beggar going from door to door.

I was thinking that maybe I'd get a maid
Find a place nearby for her to stay.
Just someone to keep my house clean,
Fix my meals and go away.

A maid. A man needs a maid.
A maid.

It's hard to make that change
When life and love turn strange.
And cold.

To live a love, you gotta give a love.
To give a love, you gotta be part of.
When will I see you again?

A while ago somewhere I don't know when
I was watching a movie with a friend.
I fell in love with the actress.
She was playing a part that I could understand.

A maid. A man needs a maid.
A maid.
When will I see you again?

He objectifies the actress he falls in love with. She is just someone who is playing "a part that he can understand." That is good enough for him in his loneliness. Another maid he can hire.

On the matter of objectification we have Don Henley's "bubble headed bleach blonde who comes on at five." Just someone. A cliché, but she's good enough at what she does.

Dirty Laundry, Don Henley

I make my living off the evening news
Just give me something, something I can use
People love it when you lose, they love dirty laundry

Well, I could've been an actor, but I wound up here
I just have to look good, I don't have to be clear
Come and whisper in my ear, give us dirty laundry

Kick 'em when they're up, kick 'em when they're down
Kick 'em when they're up, kick 'em when they're down
Kick 'em when they're up, kick 'em when they're down
Kick 'em when they're up, kick 'em all around

We got the bubble-headed bleach-blonde who comes on at five
She can tell you 'bout the plane crash with a gleam in her eye
It's interesting when people die, give us dirty laundry

Can we film the operation? Is the head dead yet?
You know the boys in the newsroom got a running bet
Get the widow on the set, we need dirty laundry

You don't really need to find out what's going on
You don't really want to know just how far it's gone
Just leave well enough alone, keep your dirty laundry

Dirty little secrets, dirty little lies
We got our dirty little fingers in everybody's pie
Love to cut you down to size, we love dirty laundry

We can do the innuendo, we can dance and sing
When it's said and done, we haven't told you a thing
We all know that crap is king, give us dirty laundry

And there is objectification again in the widow who is to be used as a prop for the evening news. Is her husband's head dead yet? "Get the widow on the set."

George Jones is bereft, desperately lonely. He deludes himself. Or not. Maybe he knows he is lying to himself:

<u>She thinks I still care, George Jones</u>

Just because I ask a friend about her
Just because I spoke her name somewhere
Just because I rang her number by mistake today
She thinks I still care.

Just because I haunt the same old places
Where the mem'ry of her lingers ev'rywhere
Just because I'm not the happy guy I used to be
She thinks I still care.

But if she's happy thinkin' I still need her
Then let that silly notion bring her cheer
But how could she ever be so foolish
Oh, where would she get such an idea.
Just because I ask a friend about her
Just because I spoke her name somewhere
Just because I saw her then went all to pieces
She thinks I still care.

In 1955 the Platters released "The Great Pretender," with lyrics written in the washroom of the Las Vegas Flamingo Hotel by Buck Ram. It became The Platters' first national #1 hit.

It is a painful orgy of self-analysis. It is embarrassing. It screams of isolation, loneliness. Like George Jones, the male lead sings, "You've left me to dream all alone."

<u>The Platters, The Great Pretender</u>

Oh yes I'm the great pretender
Pretending that I'm doing well
My need is such I pretend too much
I'm lonely but no one can tell

Oh yes I'm the great pretender
Adrift in a world of my own
I play the game but to my real shame
You've left me to dream all alone

Too real is this feeling of make believe
Too real when I feel what my heart can't conceal
Ooh Ooh yes I'm the great pretender
Just laughing and gay like a clown
I seem to be what I'm not (you see)
I'm wearing my heart like a crown
Pretending that you're still around
Yeah ooh hoo

His real love is gone. She has left him, and he is keeping up appearances.

FAHRENHEIT 451

I knew the title referred to the temperature at which books burn. I just knew it would be a riff on how bad the Nazis were, about their burning of "Jewish" books.

But it is not. *Fahrenheit 451* is Ray Bradbury's 1953 book about people struggling against or succumbing to state control. As in Orwell's *1984*, the people are believable. We care about them. They hold our interest. We want to know how they turn out. We must read the book to the end.

Mildred is the saddest person in *Fahrenheit 451*. She is Guy Montag's wife. She wants to watch screens all the time. Those are whole walls in a dedicated room of their house. The Montags have additionally purchased the ability of the screens to recognize them, to talk to them, to involve them in the "family" which populates the walls.

The screens substitute for real life, for a real family, for going outside the house, for finding buttercups, for conversation with people who don't care about screens. The screens must exist in a world with no books, no radio, no television, no learning extrinsic to the screens. They fill a need. The state provides through the walls what it believes the people need.

The walls are expensive. It appears that everybody has one wall, but many upgrade to two, three, or even four walls. They do this at their own expense. The Montags have three walls. Mildred wants four. Montag says they don't have enough money.

Montag burns books. It is his job. He is a fireman, a "Salamander," following in what we are told Benjamin Franklin did. Franklin, we are told, was the first fireman and the first book burner. Now and then Montag does not burn a book. He keeps it. That is illegal. He brings it home and hides it. Then he meets a girl, Clarice, who makes him think. This is a turn of plot parallel to Winston meeting Julia in *1984*.

Fahrenheit 451 does not lecture. It shows. But authors are not always so wise. Unfortunately, Aldous Huxley's *Brave New World* is a lecture from beginning to end. It is a diatribe against state control. Huxley made that choice. Huxley's people are not interesting, and so we do not read the book to the end.

Ayn Rand's *Anthem* does not lecture. It shows. We care about what happens to the numbered man we meet and the numbered woman he falls in love with. We have to read to the end.

Montag is headed down a dangerous road. We care about what happens to him. We have to read *Fahrenheit 451* to the end.

GLOBAL WARMING

Let us consider three facts:

1. Global warming is happening now.
2. Our planet has always gone through cycles of warming and cooling.
3. There is now a large industry devoted to the idea that global warming is caused by man.

The geological record shows a persistent 1500-year cycle of warming and cooling extending back at least 1 million years. This cycle happened and happens with or without the humans we know today: Those driving automobiles, air conditioning their homes and offices, and flying jet planes with massive exhausts.

Nevertheless, it is plausible that humans could contribute to the warming of the climate. We cannot dismiss that idea. We know that the burning of fossil fuels releases CO_2 into the atmosphere. We know that the level of carbon dioxide in the atmosphere has been growing steadily since the beginning of the Industrial Revolution. CO_2 is called a "greenhouse-gas," meaning that it strongly absorbs infrared heat radiation from the sun. So the idea of an enhanced greenhouse effect is to be looked at straight on.

We need to remember that CO2 is a plant food. It is indispensable to life on the planet. Plants absorb CO2. They need it for their own growth. The plants then release oxygen into the atmosphere.

We often hear that there is a "consensus" of scientists that human activity causes global warming. However, this is not how science works. Scientific advancements usually come from a minority challenging the majority view, sometimes even a single person. Einstein and Galileo come to mind. Science proceeds from conclusions based on evidence, not on a show of hands.

There is a mitigation industry now. Subsidies for "green" products abound. For wind energy. For solar panels. For electric cars. For triple-insulated windows. Authors who subscribe to the "consensus" get their articles published, their reputations enhanced, their careers advanced.

The entire mitigation industry is an admirable, entrepreneurial chasing-of-the dollar. After all, if somebody is giving money away, why not get in line? Lyndon Johnson came to Knoxville in the sixties. In a speech he robustly declared "war on poverty." A wag in the crowd shouted, "Hell, I surrender." If somebody is giving money away, get in line.

SHOT AND GAUGES

The smallest shot is number 12. This shot is tiny. I believe they are used only in .22 long rifle cartridges. They take the place of the bullet which would normally be there. When the cartridge is fired the tiny shot fly out and travel not very far and not very fast. When they hit a bear, the bear notices it simply as a smack on his pelt. The tiny shot cannot penetrate his pelt. The bear reacts chiefly to the noise and the smoke. He runs away.

Shot sizes range up gradually from number 12 until they reach double 00 buckshot. These shot are large. In a 12-gauge shotgun shell there will only be nine of them. They are of course deadly.

Shotgun gauges are an historical artifact. The gauge of a shotgun equals the number of lead balls fitting that shotgun necessary to equal one pound of lead. A 12-gauge shotgun requires twelve such balls. And so on for the 10-gauge, the 16-gauge, the 20-gauge, and the 28-gauge. Curiously, a small shotgun, the .410, is named by its bore diameter expressed in inches.

There are other gauges, but they are rare. The 11, 15, 18, 2, and 3-gauge shells are rarest of all. In the early 1900s there was a 14-gauge, but no more. There still are very small

24 and 32 gauges produced and used in some European and South American countries.

There is a handgun named "The Judge." I wish it were not so named. Taurus makes it. It is a miserable piece of weaponry, consisting of two chambers, one for a 45-caliber cartridge, the other for a .410 shotgun shell. Shooting it is worse than going to the dentist. If it doesn't sprain your hand, you've been lucky. However, it is probably the ultimate in home protection if you can stand to own it.

HITLER ON GUNS

"This year will go down in history. For the first time, a civilized nation has full gun registration. Our streets will be safer, our police more efficient, and the world will follow our lead into the future!"
--Adolph Hitler, 1935

FAUST II

Faust II (1832) is a mess. Goethe turned it loose in the last year of his life. He should not have.

He should have rested happily on *Faust I* (1805), which is a masterpiece. But no, he slathered together a number of vague pompous concepts and presumed we would accept their validity. For example, *"Das ewig weibliche zieht uns hinan."* (*"The eternally feminine draws us upward."*) What horse manure.

Just because you are a writer of stature does not mean you are infallible. Fallibility apparently did not occur to Goethe.

PALETTE

The multiple choices we have in any given minute are a palette of choices. An artist's board of colored paints, or flowers, or flavors. But a palette can be a range of tasks. That is one of its dangerous iterations. That palette has the crushing effect of sequencing. What comes first? In what order do I do my tasks? What should come first?

This palette is the hairball of the driven life. Rushing, jamming things into our day, living the life of self-condemnation. There is a huge potential for evil hidden in this palette. We must break the sequencing, break the line-up of tasks. How?

Well, it turns out that it's easy: We take our palette knife and scrape entire colors off the board. We remove parts of the 'necessaries.' This then gives us more time for pausing, for contemplation, for reflection. With me a case in point was not running for reelection. Lately it is often the decision not to undertake a large task today, but to save it for later.

When I have this good sense, I am insisting on quality instead of quantity. I am rejecting a jammed-up sequence, the succession of 'necessary' things I earlier lined up as needful to self-worth. Instead, I opt for time to think, to pause, to reflect, to pray, to contemplate. To enjoy what is here now, to cherish the moment. This is a turning away from the received need to produce.

You might say that the driving of self is the handiwork of a force which does not want us to pause, which does not want us to contemplate God's glory, which does not want us to dwell on how we might help others today. I believe there is a force which does not want us to be rooted, blessed, gathered in, ensconced, enfolded in grace. I believe we live surrounded by a force which wants us to be driven, rushed, concerned for what is to come next in our sequencing of tasks.

But with a simple stepping-away to this question: "What if I were to die today?" we change our monoscope to an entire worldview. The earlier railroad of milestones becomes a moment of sun and green leaves, the echo of a locomotive whistle dancing in the hills. "If I die today, this is where I die, in this moment of beauty." This is the moment of beauty which Faust believed would never come. He was so sure of it, he bet his soul on it.

Jamming-up is destruction. It may be unconscious, but it is not fleeting. Jamming-up sneaks in unquestioned. It demands you be serious, responsible. It demands you heed the values you long ago internalised. And so you live a prescription not knowing that it is just that, a written mandate. A cat does not do this. A cat walks from moment to moment seeing and enjoying.

We should savor the slow changes of seasons. Savor the moments, savor our every glimpse of this one day today. Take it in. Do not think ahead to what must be done, what is yet to do. It will take care of itself. Approach the undone with prayer.

PEARLS

The problem is joy or the absence of it. The problem is taking one step at a time, as C.S. Lewis suggests, when the problems of the day come rushing at us. When we awake we have the moment to decide how the day will be. Will it be a succession of necessities, or the opposite? Will it be joy savored? Or will it be a lecture that things will be well only if we do a penance? How do we begin the day?

What to do when those tasks come rushing? How about pausing and thinking about the situation? Realizing that you are about to be robbed of God's given grace? That you are about to be robbed of being in God's creation all around you. You can ignore that opportunity, and even be praised for doing so, because you chose to be devoted to task.

So, you can avoid beauty and contemplation at the start of the day, and at sixty-six other junctures today. Or you can take the other path, the gradual path, the path that leads you know not where, but be fully present in each of its moments. This is not disorganization.

If we do that, we will have a string of pearls, each enjoyed and examined. We will not know, you and I, what the next pearl is to be. We will wait and see. At the end of the day we will have a string of those pearls but we will probably not remember each one, nor know how long the string is.

At the end of the day we will have the joy of looking back and saying, "Yes, God has done all that." But even as we look back and total them up, the pearls, will we then ask ourselves, "Yes, but can I do it again tomorrow?"

No. At the end of the day of that string of pearls we will have peace and look forward to new pearls, whatever they may be. As I write this, I am describing a day of wonder. As I write this, I am comfortable with that description. I believe that tomorrow will be a day of blessedness, of grace and joy. Let us see, you and I.

HOW CHILDREN PLAYED BUTCHERING

This is tough stuff. The brothers Grimm faithfully collected (often in dialect) the stories parents told their children-- good, bad, indifferent, charming, or horrible. The first edition came out in 1812, the seventh and last in 1857. Many of them are our favorites today. For example, Cinderella and Hansel and Gretel. Here is one which is not. But the brothers Grimm faithfully catalogued even this horrible story, and here it is.

"Wie Kinder Schlachtens miteinander gespielt haben" ("How Children Played Butchering with Each Other") is one of two slaughtering stories the brothers collected. Here is the second and shorter of the two stories.

Once upon a time a father slaughtered a pig. His children watched. That afternoon as they were playing, one of them said to the other: "You will be the little pig, and I will be the butcher," took a naked knife and stuck into his little brother's neck. The mother, who was bathing her youngest child upstairs in a tub, heard the scream of her other child, ran immediately downstairs, and when she saw what had happened, pulled the knife out of the neck of the child and stuck it in anger into the heart of the child who had been the butcher.

Then she immediately ran back to the room and wanted to see what her baby was doing in the tub, but it had meanwhile drowned in the bath; as a result she became so full of anxiety that she despaired, would not let herself be comforted by her servants, but rather hanged herself. Her husband came back from the field and when he had seen all this, he became so depressed, that shortly thereafter he died.

Here it is in the original:

Einstmals hat ein Hausvater ein Schwein geschlachtet, das haben seine Kinder gesehen; als sie nun Nachmittag miteinander spielen wollen, hat das eine Kind zum andern gesagt: »du sollst das Schweinchen und ich der Metzger sein«, hat darauf ein bloß Messer genommen, und es seinem Brüderchen in den Hals gestoßen. Die Mutter, welche oben in der Stube saß und ihr jüngstes Kindlein in einem Zuber badete, hörte das Schreien ihres anderen Kindes, lief alsbald hinunter, und als sie sah, was vorgegangen, zog sie das Messer dem Kind aus dem Hals und stieß es im Zorn, dem andern Kind, welches der Metzger gewesen, ins Herz. Darauf lief sie alsbald nach der Stube und wollte sehen, was ihr Kind in dem Badezuber mache, aber es war unterdessen in dem Bad ertrunken; deswegen dann die Frau so voller Angst ward, dass sie in Verzweiflung geriet, sich von ihrem Gesinde nicht wollte trösten lassen, sondern sich selbst erhängte. Der Mann kam vom Felde und als er dies alles gesehen, hat er sich so betrübt, dass er kurz darauf gestorben ist.

The Grimm Cinderella story is also rugged, but it has been sanitized for Disney audiences. In the original version the two stepsisters are able to put the slipper on (the one Cinderella lost at the palace). The first sister does it by cutting off her big toe with her mother's help. The prince takes the sister up upon his horse and rides away, but before he gets to the palace he sees the blood and brings her back. The second sister has no toe problem, but her heel is too big. Her mother tells her to cut off part of her heel, because after all when she is queen she will not need to walk. After a bit, the prince brings her back as well.

--Grimm, Wilhelm Carl; Jacob Ludwig Carl Grimm,*Grimms Märchen, Vollständig überarbeitete und illustrierte Ausgabe speziell für digitale Lesegeräte* (German Edition) (Kindle Locations 2968-2976). Null Papier Verlag. Kindle Edition.

THE 23RD PSALM

King James bible, 1611:

The LORD is my shepherd; I shall not want.
He maketh me to lie down in green pastures: he leadeth me beside the still waters.
He restoreth my soul: he leadeth me in the paths of righteousness for his name's sake.
Yea, though I walk through the valley of the shadow of death, I will fear no evil: for thou art with me; thy rod and thy staff they comfort me.
Thou preparest a table before me in the presence of mine enemies: thou anointest my head with oil; my cup runneth over.
Surely goodness and mercy shall follow me all the days of my life: and I will dwell in the house of the LORD for ever.

The Hebrew Bible, Robert Alter, 2019:

The Lord is my shepherd, I shall not want.
In grass meadows He makes me lie down,
by quiet waters guides me.
My life He brings back.
He leads me on pathways of justice for His name's sake.

143

Though I walk in the vale of death's shadow,
I fear no harm, for You are with me.
Your rod and Your staff--it is they that console me.
You set out a table before me in the face of my foes.
You moisten my head with oil, my cup overflows.
Let but goodness and kindness pursue me
all the days of my life.
And I shall dwell in the house of the Lord
for many long days.

The theme of the shepherd and his flock is recurrent in the old and new testaments. It is to the shepherds outside Bethlehem that the good news is first brought, "For unto you is born this day in the city of David a Savior, who is Christ the Lord."

Isaiah tells the people of Israel in chapter 40, "Behold, the Lord comes with might and his arm rules for him; behold his reward is with him, and his recompense before him. He will tend to his flock like a shepherd, he will gather the lambs in his arms; he will carry them in his bosom, and gently lead those that are with young."

In Luke 15 the Pharisees and scribes grumble that Jesus is spending time with sinners, even eating with them. Christ tells them a parable about a shepherd who has lost one of his sheep. The shepherd goes after the one who is lost, and when he finds it, he lays it on his shoulders, rejoicing. "Just so," Christ says, "there will be more joy in heaven over one sinner who repents than over ninety-nine righteous persons who need no repentance."

John gives us Christ's words in chapter 10: "I am the good shepherd and I know my own, and my own know me. I am the door. If anyone enters by me, he will be saved and will go in and out and find pasture."

SNOWMEN DISCUSS INTELLIGENT DESIGN

King James Bible, 1611
Psalm 100, verse 3: *Know ye that the LORD he is God:*

It is he that hath made us, and not we ourselves;

We are his people, and the sheep of his pasture.

New International Version Bible, 1973
Psalm 100, verse 3: *Know that the LORD is God.*

It is he who made us, and we are his; we are his people, the sheep of his pasture.

Robert Alter, <u>The Hebrew Bible</u>, 2019
Psalm 100, verse 3: *Know that the Lord is God.*
He has made us, and we are His,
His people and the flock He tends.

Intelligent Design presents two main arguments against evolutionary explanations: irreducible complexity and specified complexity, asserting that certain biological and informational features of living things are too complex to be the result of natural selection.

Irreducible complexity is the argument that certain biological systems cannot have evolved by successive small modifications to pre-existing functional systems through natural selection, because no less complex system would function.

William Paley argued, in his 1802 watchmaker analogy, that complexity in nature implies a God for the same reason that the existence of a watch implies the existence of a watchmaker. This argument has a long history, and one can trace it back at least as far as Cicero's *De Natura Deorum* ii.34, written in 45 BC.

SEVEN SMALL
IMPERFECTIONS

We encounter small imperfections every day. Usually we do not notice them enough even to say, "Oh, my goodness, look at that. How unfortunate."

But we do notice large imperfections. They stop us in our tracks. Mass shootings, hurricanes, the Down Syndrome child. We hurt and we ponder. We pray and we think. We want to make the large imperfections go away. We want to think them away, pray them away.

Sometimes the large and terrible things are gateways to small good things. Gratitude for the life of the shooting victim, memories of her goodness. A resolution to treat everyone as though it might just be our last chance.

Even in the wake of hurricanes we rejoice in helpers' countless acts of kindness. We admire the sister at Walmart shopping with her fifty-six- year-old Down Syndrome sister.

I describe here not a Pollyanna response, but an active self-defense perhaps. It is, I think, our grasping for the good. It is our hoping for the good. It is our certain knowledge that our God is not the god of suffering but of salvation. He does not rejoice in evil. He sees it and grieves beside us.

The problem of evil, of bad things happening, has been addressed by theology for centuries. We do not daily walk the road of theological examination. We simply focus on our belief in goodness, on our devotion to goodness, our preference for perfection. We do not need Aquinas to tell us that we hurt and that there are no clear answers.

There is however one area where we can, I think, make tangible hands-on progress. It is in the small imperfections. These small slings and arrows wound too, but less than the large imperfections. The small hurts are around us every day, many times a day--the cut finger, the dented fender, the bad attorney who bilks his client, gross language spoken by others or by us, the politician we once admired who has turned against his party's president, the president who is sometimes politically inept, our own undergraduate school which has become a leftist cesspool. These things--and there are many more--wound us by their frequency, by their aggregate drip, drip, drip.

The cut finger—there is little we can do for it but keep it dry, bandage it, and be glad it was not worse. That is in fact a small blessing. It wasn't an artery. No stitches were needed.

The dented fender we can bandage with money.

The bad attorney can be reported to the state board of professional responsibility.

We can simply stop our own bad language, and let the gross language of others be an object lesson for us.

The politician we admired who attacks his party's president can be regretted, avoided, and voted out of office.

The president who commits a gaffe can be at least admired for his naivete. A breath of fresh air. Jimmy Carter admitted to having adulterous thoughts.

Our own college being held hostage by leftism really wounds, standing as a representative of the decline of American values. Our response is not to bemoan the loss of Harvard, but to persuade it to a better path. We do not stay silent, even if we know we cannot perceptibly change the poor benighted place. Harvard was gloriously present at the founding of America. It now urges the foundering of America.

These seven small imperfections stand for seventy more we will meet this week and for seven thousand more we will meet this year. All these imperfections are small but, yes, they are wearing.

So our thirst for perfection makes us register these flaws and try to cope with them. The imperfections assault our peace; they wear down our sense of well-being. When we try to be present in the moment, try to be thankful, try to be grateful, try to be open to beauty, the imperfections drag us back to dullness. It is Mozart played from a scratched record. The music itself becomes flawed. We cannot unhear the scratch. A once perfect dinner plate now has a nick in its edge. We cannot unsee it.

Where do we go from here? We might perhaps go with Polly and her sister Anna. We might tell ourselves over and over that there are worse things than a life filled with small imperfections. That is poor comfort, yes, but it is something. It is a plan.

MARY, DID YOU KNOW?

If you do not know this Christmas carol, get ready for a treat. Try the version of it done *a cappella* by Pentatonix:

> *Mary, did you know*
> *that your Baby Boy would one day walk on water?*
> *Mary, did you know*
> *that your Baby Boy would save our sons and daughters?*
> *Did you know*
> *that your Baby Boy has come to make you new?*
> *This Child that you delivered will soon deliver you?*

This is quite a change of perspective from our usual all-centeredness as consumers of Christ's coming ("*Oh come, all ye faithful, joyful and triumphant . . .*") to Mary's perspective, to thinking about Mary's view of the event.

> *Mary, did you know*
> *that your Baby Boy will give sight to a blind man?*
> *Mary, did you know*
> *that your Baby Boy will calm the storm with His hand?*
> *Did you know*
> *that your Baby Boy has walked where angels trod?*
> *When you kiss your little Baby you kiss the face of God?*

And, Mary, how about this:

> *Did you know*
> *that your Baby Boy is heaven's perfect Lamb?*
> *The sleeping Child you're holding is the Great, I Am.*

We know Mary has been through the Annunciation (Luke 1:26) and has spent three months with Elizabeth, who is carrying John the Baptist, but now her own baby boy is here! The one foretold.

What is she thinking? Does she have foreknowledge of what is to come? And if she does, she sees the crucifixion already, the baby boy in her arms, nailed and dead. It is merciful the carol does not take us there. But we think of it, of her wonder, of her joy, of her coming grief.

This carol is not some Catholic church veneration-of-Mary argument. It is a song for her, about her foreknowledge perhaps, about her fears. About her wonder certainly.

But it is also about our own wonder, our own grief, our foreknowledge.

PINK FLOYD: ON THE TURNING AWAY

1987, Pink Floyd released *On the Turning Away*, part of his album *A Momentary Lapse of Reason*. I hold it to be a deeply Christian song. Here is the first stanza:

> *On the turning away*
> *From the pale and downtrodden*
> *And the words they say*
> *Which we won't understand:*
> *"Don't accept that what's happening*
> *Is just a case of others' suffering*
> *Or you'll find that you're joining in*
> *The turning away."*

Stanzas two and four tell us:

Driven on by a heart of stone,
We could find that we're all alone
In the dream of the proud.
No more turning away
From the weak and the weary
No more turning away

Just a world that we all must share.
It's not enough just to stand and stare.
Is it only a dream that there'll be
No more turning away?

Let us hope that it is not only a dream. We must accept and share others' burdens. Help them prosper. Lead them.

THE GATLINBURG FIRE

On 23 November 2016, two juveniles were "playing with matches" on the trail to the Chimney Tops in the Great Smoky Mountains National Park. They caused a wildfire as a result. In a few days, high winds drove hundreds of flaming fire bombs eastward into the park and north towards Gatlinburg and Pigeon Forge. Fourteen people died. Millions of dollars of property burned.

There can be no doubt that the juveniles lacked the necessary mental intent, what the law calls *mens rea*, to achieve those particular results. Nevertheless, those are exactly the results they achieved. The Fourth Judicial District Attorney General for Sevier County, James Dunn, suppressed the names of the individuals, and refused to allow them to be prosecuted under criminal law as adults.

So much for the criminal law. Unfortunately however, the suppression of the names additionally prevented the juveniles and their parents from being identified and pursued in civil lawsuits under tort law.

If they had been identified, discovery could then have ensued to find out whether there were facts to support parental liability. It is unlikely that sufficient facts would emerge for parental liability to attach in Tennessee, but that is not the point. The point is there could be no discovery, and was no discovery.

When a child is engaged in a so-called "adult activity," he may be held to the same standard of care as an adult. That means if the child fails to live up to the adult standard of reasonable behavior and causes another person's injury, simply being a juvenile won't prevent him from being liable for that person's injuries.

Was the striking of matches an "adult activity"? It would seem so. If that is so, the child may be held to the same duty of care as an adult. The child and/or his parents may be considered liable for another person's injury or loss. The fact that he was a minor will not protect him/his parents from liability.

Under Tennessee Code section 37-10-101, a corporation, county, town, village, school district, or state entity--in addition to individuals--may collect damages from a minor's parents.

A parent's liability under section 37-10-102 is limited to $10,000, plus reimbursement of the claimant's costs of bringing the claim to court.

This $10,000 amount is limited to "actual damages." These are the out-of-court expenses associated with the injury or property damage. For example, if an individual suffered an injury, the "actual damages" would be the amount of medical bills the individual incurred in relation to the injury. "Actual damages" does not include non-economic damages, such as "pain and suffering."

Under Tennessee Code Title 37, Chapter 10, Part 1, parents and legal guardians can be held financially responsible if a minor child in their custody <u>maliciously or willfully</u> causes personal injury or property damage.

"Willful" is a legal term of art that means a person intended to take a specific action, and may have even intended a specific result. It is a heightened standard that requires more than mere carelessness on the part of the minor. So if a minor causes a car accident in Tennessee, that is not enough to trigger a parent's liability for the resulting injuries or vehicle damage (assuming the crash really was not intentional). However, the statute would apply if a minor commits an act of vandalism or an assault and battery on someone else.

Additionally, Tennessee has codified the "Common Law" rule. Tennessee Code section 37-10-103 explains exactly when parents may be financially responsible for their child's actions even if the child's actions are not malicious or willful. It says that a parent or guardian may be liable for the activities of a minor in their control who causes personal injury or property damage if:

- the parent knows, or should know, the child has a tendency to commit wrongful acts that could be expected to cause injury and/or property damage;
- the parent has an opportunity to control the child; and
- the parent fails to exercise reasonable means to prevent the injurious activity.

A parent will be presumed to know of a child's tendency to commit wrongful acts if the child has previously been charged and found responsible for such actions.

Suppose a parent knows that his child comes home from school each day and throws rocks at houses around the neighborhood. In that situation, the parent knows that the child has a tendency to commit a tortious activity which could be expected to cause personal injury or property damage. If the parent fails to exercise reasonable means to prevent his child from throwing rocks at houses in the neighborhood, and the minor then damages someone's property, or hurts someone with a thrown rock, there is a good chance the parent will be responsible for the damages that result.

LICKSPITTLE

One day walking at Lakeshore Park I was passed by two friends. They asked if I was writing a third book. I said that I was. They asked what it was going to be about. I said, "Things that piss me off." Now whenever we meet at Lakeshore, they immediately throw their hands up in the air and shout, "Things that piss me off!"

Well, here is one of them. I call it "lickspittle" because of the final sentence in this recusal. I think as you read it you will see why.

IN THE FOURTH CIRCUIT COURT FOR KNOX COUNTY, TENNESSEE

SHARON D. HAJKO

VS

NO. 71355

CHARLES V. HAJKO

ORDER OF RECUSAL

This case is an action for divorce. All issues of fault, equitable distribution, and spousal support are presently scheduled for trial 30 November 1999. The undersigned recuses himself from further consideration of contested matters in this cause, due to the action of the Court of Appeals 17 August 1999.

The parties shall immediately apply to the Honorable Mary Beth Leibowitz, presiding judge for the Sixth Judicial District, for the appointment of an interchange judge from one of the other nine local courts of record. If local interchange is not possible, the parties shall immediately pursue with the presiding judge the possibility of an interchange judge from a contiguous county. If no such judge is available, the parties shall immediately request the presiding judge to obtain a judge by designation from Ms. Suzanne Keith, Administrative Office of the Courts.

Captain Hajko was incarcerated by the undersigned 13 August 1999 for civil contempt.

The Court of Appeals reversed this court 17 August 1999, releasing Captain Hajko from incarceration, and restoring to him the funds escrowed from the marital estate. The Court of Appeals found that this judge "had so departed from the accepted and usual course of judicial proceedings as to require immediate review." A short history of the case is appropriate to this recusal.

Prior to Captain Hajko's incarceration, the case had been through repeated laborious efforts to compel discovery of Captain Hajko's financial affairs. At Trial Management Conference 7 May 1999 counsel informed the court of a "paper trail of securities" which had not yet been unraveled, and of a "confusion of documents" relating to the parties' marital possessions. Trial was reset to 30 November 1999.

On 21 May 1999, Mrs. Hajko had moved the court

for an order dividing the on-going proceeds of the husband's military retirement payment. For cause, the Plaintiff would show that the husband receives military retirement in the amount of approximately $2,000.00 per month; that the military pension represents a marital asset for which the wife is receiving no benefit; that the trial of this cause has been continued from May 11, 1999, to November 30, 1999, and should the Court not divide the pension payments for this period of time she will realize a loss of approximately $6,000.00.

In anticipation of an argument that the husband is unemployed and is using the pension to live on and pay.child support with, the Plaintiff would show that the husband is willfully unemployed and that he lives with his girlfriend who is either assisting with his living expenses or in fact supporting him.

For these and other reasons, the Plaintiff would respectfully move this Court for an Order equally dividing the pension payments received.from the husband's military retirement pending trial of this cause.

On 28 May 1999 at hearing in open court with both counsel and both parties present, this court held that Captain Hajko was voluntarily under-employed, and ordered Captain Hajko to escrow the marital portion of his military pension in a trust account held by the two attorneys, for disbursal to the parties subject to possible agreed order of counsel, or further order of the court after an additional hearing.

On 18 June Mrs. Hajko moved the Court for formal entry of the order from 28 May, the entry of which had been delayed by husband's counsel:

On May 28, 1999, the Court ordered the Defendant to place the marital portion of his retirement income into an interest bearing escrow account to be controlled by the signature of both Counsel in this cause. Subsequently, Plaintiff's Counsel sent Defendant's Counsel a letter suggesting three banks to use said funds pending further Order of the disposition of this matter, however, since that time there has been no response. from Defendant's Counsel and Plaintiff does not know where the funds are, who is holding the funds, or whether or not they have been dissipated.

Accompanying the aforementioned letter was a proposed Order from the May 28 hearing, however, as of the date of the filing of this Motion, there has been no response back on the adequacy of said letter from Defendant's Counsel. Plaintiff would show that an Order should be immediately entered so as to preserve her rights and to seek enforcement of the Order if necessary.

Captain Hajko did not deposit the marital portion of his pension funds. On 22 July 1999 Mrs. Hajko requested an immediate attachment of his body; the setting of an appearance bond; and trial of the contempt issues after the posting of bond. The undersigned, after argument, instead on 22 July issued an order to Captain Hajko to appear and show cause why the refusal should not be deemed contemptuous.

The hearing was duly held **22 days later** on 13 August 1999, which was **77 days after the court had ordered Captain Hajko in open court to deposit the marital portion of his military pension.** At that hearing the court found, and placed in its order the finding, that Captain Hajko continued to be under-employed as an "insurance salesman"; that the court did not unreservedly accept his "heavy" clothing costs, nor "eating out" costs as appropriate business expenses; that Mrs. Hajko was working three jobs to feed herself and her children; that Captain Hajko was living in adultery with a person sharing his living expenses; that it was Captain Hajko's intent to reduce his wife to abject penury; and that Captain Hajko had no intention of respecting the orders of the trial court as to preservation of the marital estate.

He was incarcerated for willful contempt, in that he had not deposited the marital portion of his military pension in an escrow account as ordered.

The Court of Appeals received the telephone argument of counsel, and reviewed no transcript. The Court of Appeals could not see that Captain Hajko is handsome, able-bodied, highly articulate, and extraordinarily bright. The Court of Appeals did not have the benefit of observing Captain Hajko's arrogant, sneering demeanor in court, nor his paramour seated in the front row of the gallery.

But the Court of Appeals, after telephone argument, ratified Captain Hajko's contemptuous conduct, and in so doing took from Mrs. Hajko any possibility of asset preservation by this court. She has become the vassal of her husband henceforth, a woman who may accept on her knees the leavings from his table, should there be any. It is difficult to see how this constitutes appropriate interlocutory oversight by the Tennessee Court of Appeals.

In the hope that there may be a judge somewhere whose orders Captain Hajko will follow, a judge whose asset preservation orders the Court of Appeals will affirm, the undersigned recuses himself. A withdrawal by this judge must happen now because Mrs. Hajko can hereafter receive no justice at the hands of the undersigned. This judge has become powerless. Captain Hajko can hereafter--and given his prior conduct will hereafter--ignore with impunity any orders issuing from the undersigned, whom the Court of Appeals has converted to lickspittle.

IT IS SO ORDERED.

ENTER this twentieth day of August 1999.

_____
JUDGE BILL SWANN

CERTIFICATE

I hereby certify that a true and exact copy of the foregoing has been hand-delivered to The Honorable Mary Beth Leibowitz, City County Building, Knoxville, TN 37902; forwarded by US mail to Douglas J. Toppenberg, Esq., 612 Gay Street, Suite #1, and Robert R. Simpson, 1776 Riverview Tower, 900 S. Gay Street, Knoxville, TN 37902, this 20th day of August 1999.

_____
JUDGE BILL SWANN, by jm

JONES V. RUSCH-JONES

This is a case I tried in 2007. It lasted twenty-five days, and it was then appealed to the state court of appeals. It will give you an idea of how hard a trial court judge works, and how hard the civil court of appeals works.

IN THE COURT OF APPEALS OF TENNESSEE
AT KNOXVILLE
May 17, 2007 Session

THOMAS R. JONES, JR. v. HEATHER L. RUSCH-JONES

Appeal from the Fourth Circuit Court for Knox County Nos. 97520 & 97555 Bill Swann, Judge

No. E2006-01998-COA-R3-CV - FILED JULY 19, 2007

Following a short marriage of less than four years, Thomas R. Jones, Jr. ("Father") filed a complaint for divorce from Heather L. Rusch-Jones ("Mother"). Mother filed a counter-claim also seeking a divorce. Both parties sought to be the primary residential parent of their young daughter. While this case was pending, both parties filed competing petitions for orders of protection. Father's petition was granted; Mother's was not. Following a very lengthy trial, the Trial Court designated Father as the primary residential parent and awarded Mother supervised and restricted co-parenting time. The Trial Court awarded Mother a limited amount of alimony. Mother appeals raising numerous issues, including a challenge to the Trial Court's designation of Father as the primary residential parent and the amount of alimony she was awarded. We affirm the judgment of the Trial Court and remand for further proceedings consistent with this Opinion.

Tenn. R. App. P. 3 Appeal as of Right; Judgment of the Fourth Circuit Court Affirmed; Case Remanded

D. MICHAEL SWINEY, J., delivered the opinion of the court, in which SHARON G. LEE, J., joined. CHARLES D. SUSANO, JR., J., filed a separate concurring opinion.

John D. Lockridge and Sammi S. Maifair, Knoxville, Tennessee, for the Appellant, Heather L. Rusch-Jones.

Virginia A. Schwamm and Donna H. Smith, Knoxville, Tennessee, for the Appellee, Thomas R. Jones, Jr.

OPINION

Background

This is an appeal from an exceptionally contentious divorce proceeding. The parties were married in July of 2000 and have a daughter who was born in March of 2003. Father filed a complaint for divorce in June of 2004 alleging Mother was guilty of inappropriate marital conduct or, in the alternative, that irreconcilable differences had arisen between the parties. Father sought to be designated as the child's primary residential parent.

Mother answered the complaint and denied that she had engaged in any inappropriate marital conduct. Mother filed a counter-complaint seeking a divorce claiming Father had engaged in inappropriate marital conduct or, alternatively, that there were irreconcilable differences between the parties. Mother likewise sought to be designated as the child's primary residential parent.

There were numerous court proceedings involving temporary custody and temporary support issues and the like before the trial. There also were issues surrounding competing petitions for orders of protection filed by both parties. The Trial Court entered an order of protection against Mother and ordered Mother to pay Father's attorney fees incurred in the prosecution of the order of protection. Mother's request for an order of protection against Father was denied. Mother also filed two motions to recuse during the course of these proceedings. Both of these motions were denied.

Following a lengthy trial, the Trial Court issued an extensive memorandum opinion from the bench which, when transcribed, is over seventy-five pages in length. Both parties filed post-trial motions and the final judgment later was amended. The end result was that the Trial Court declared the parties divorced from each other pursuant to Tenn. Code Ann. § 36-4-129, after finding both parties had established grounds for divorce. The Trial Court designated Father as the child's [1] primary residential parent. Because the Trial Court found Mother to have some psychological issues, Mother was awarded limited and supervised co-parenting time. The Trial Court made the property distribution. The Trial Court refused to award Mother any rehabilitative alimony. The Trial Court allowed Father and the child to remain in the marital residence. Mother was ordered to vacate the marital residence immediately and Father was required to pay for Mother to stay in a hotel for one week as transitional alimony. The Trial Court awarded to Mother as alimony in solido an amount equal to one-half of the total payments Father had made on his student loans during the marriage. Finally, the Trial Court noted that it had previously ordered Father to pay $7,500 toward Mother's attorney fees as alimony in solido. The Trial Court then stated that each party "shall hereafter be responsible for the remaining attorney fees that they have incurred."

Tenn. Code Ann. § 36-4-129(b) (2005) provides that the "court may, upon stipulation to or proof of any ground for divorce pursuant to § 36-4-101, grant a divorce to the party who was less at fault or, if either or both parties are entitled to a divorce, declare the parties to be divorced, rather than awarding a divorce to either party alone."

Mother appeals claiming: (1) the Trial Court erred when it failed to grant her motions for recusal; (2) the Trial Court erred when it designated Father as the child's primary residential parent; (3) the Trial Court erred in restricting her co-parenting time and in requiring her co-parenting time be supervised; (4) the Trial Court erred when it refused to award her rehabilitative alimony; (5) the Trial Court erred in the amount of transitional alimony awarded; (6) the Trial Court erred with regard to its award of attorney fees and discretionary costs; (7) the Trial Court erred when it granted Father's request for an order of protection; (8) the Trial Court erred when it made the order of protection permanent; (9) the Trial Court erred when it awarded Father attorney fees incurred in prosecution of the order of protection; (10) the Trial Court erred in the property distribution by failing to award Mother certain items of property she claims were her separate property; and (11) the Trial Court erred when it awarded Father a judgment for damages to his separate property allegedly caused by Mother. Mother also challenges two evidentiary rulings of the Trial Court.

Discussion

The factual findings of the Trial Court are accorded a presumption of correctness, and we will not overturn those factual findings unless the evidence preponderates against them. *See* Tenn. R. App. P. 13(d); *Bogan v. Bogan*, 60 S.W.3d 721, 727 (Tenn. 2001). With respect to legal issues, our review is conducted "under a pure *de novo* standard of review, according no deference to the conclusions of law made by the lower courts." *Southern Constructors, Inc. v. Loudon County Bd. Of Educ.*, 58 S.W.3d 706, 710 (Tenn. 2001).

The trial in this case lasted over twenty-five days with numerous witnesses. The most significant trial testimony was discussed in some detail in the Trial Court's detailed 75-page memorandum opinion. Given the length of the trial and the number of witnesses, we will discuss only the relevant highlights of the trial testimony and the Trial Court's findings.

Although the competing petitions for order of protection had in large part been resolved by the time of trial, they nevertheless had an impact at trial. When granting Father's petition for an order of protection, the Trial Court made specific factual findings. The Trial Court found that on one occasion Mother repeatedly hit and kicked Father and on another occasion Mother hit Father on the back. Mother generally denied engaging in such conduct, but at trial witnesses were called who testified that Mother had admitted to them that she had hit Father. In addition, at least one witness testified that Mother stated she could have Father "offed." In short, the facts do not preponderate against the Trial Court's determination that Father was the party in need of an order of protection and that it was Mother who was the physically abusive spouse.

At trial, Father requested the order of protection be modified to allow for social contact. Because the Trial Court concluded that Mother had violated the order of protection in "many instances," the Trial Court refused to modify the order of protection and instead made it permanent. The evidence does not preponderate against the findings of the Trial Court relevant to its decision to make the order of protection permanent. (Footnote 2) Therefore, we find no reversible error by the Trial Court in making the order of protection permanent.

Footnote 2: The Trial Court found "perhaps as many as 26 violations of the no-contact order ... [which] are acts of criminal contempt." The Trial Court subsumed all of Mother's violations of the order of protection into one count and sentenced her to ten days of incarceration. However, the sentence was suspended.

Mother also claims the Trial Court erred when it awarded Father his attorney fees incurred in prosecution of the order of protection. Mother further claims that her attorney should have been permitted to depose Father's counsel regarding the amount of the attorney fee that was claimed.

Tenn. Code Ann. § 36-3-617(a) (2005) provides as follows:

Protection orders - Filing costs and assistance. – (a) Notwithstanding any other provision of law to the contrary, the petitioner shall not be required to pay any filing fees, litigation taxes or any other costs associated with the filing, issuance, service or enforcement of an order of protection authorized by this part upon the filing of the petition. The judge shall assess court costs and litigation taxes at the hearing of the petition or upon dismissal of the petition. *If the court, after the hearing, issues or extends an order of protection, petitioner's court costs and attorney fees shall be assessed against the respondent.* (emphasis added)

Based on the unequivocal and mandatory language of the statute, the Trial Court properly awarded Father his attorney fees and costs incurred in the prosecution of the order of protection.

As noted, Mother claims the Trial Court erred because her attorney was not allowed to depose Father's attorney regarding the amount of attorney fees and expenses that were claimed. In response, Father correctly points out that at the hearing on Father's request for attorney fees, Mother's attorney was allowed to question Father's attorney at length about the claimed fees and expenses. Following that hearing, the Trial Court reduced the expenses sought by Father by one-half and then awarded Father a judgment for fees and expenses totaling $4,408.43. Because Mother's attorney was afforded the opportunity to question Father's attorney about the propriety of the claimed fees and expenses, we find no error in the fact that Mother's attorney was not permitted thereafter to depose Father's attorney. The amount of fees and expenses awarded to Father is affirmed.

The Trial Court found that Mother had problems with anger management and the proof at trial certainly supports this conclusion. On at least two occasions Mother got angry and left the courtroom in the middle of court proceedings and once even threw something and yelled at her own attorney. Mother claimed that she suspected Father had sexually abused the child, but there was absolutely no evidence, medical or otherwise, to support this horrific accusation. In fact, the proof was that Father was a very good father and would never harm the child. According to the Trial Court:

Dr. Freeman notes, and the Court finds, that the mother [3] played the child sexual abuse card with the pediatrician, suggesting that the child should be examined because the mother "had concerns." Nothing was found, and the Court finds that the mere suggestion of same is just an absolute impossibility ... for this father.

A neighbor testified at trial that she witnessed Mother's attempt to back into Father's car which was being driven by Father at the time. Mother later apologized to the neighbor for doing that in front of the neighbor's child. Mother told the neighbor that she had "lost it" and was "overreacting." Mother admitted to this behavior at trial. The neighbor also testified that one week after Mother and Father were married, Mother told the neighbor that she was going to divorce Father and "take him for everything he had...." The Trial Court also set forth the following testimony from the neighbor:

[Mother] told me that they fought a lot. She said that she bought a lot of things for the house, that she would buy things on sale and just buy them and store them.... She told me once that she threw the ring out the window in an argument on the way to the Biltmore, later that she did not do that, but that she had not told [Father], that she had kept it and was going to go to New Jersey and would sell it. She told me this at her house. She also said that if I were to see her in the back yard with a shovel, [I] would know where [Father] was.

Father testified that Mother told him that he would never see his daughter again and to get ready "for the custody case of your life." Mother told Dr. Freeman that Father did not spend any time at the hospital when the child was born, an assertion that was flatly contradicted by the medical records from the hospital.

During one of the parties' many arguments, Mother supposedly threw a ring at Father which later could not be found. Father had given Mother a valuable ring and it was this ring that Mother allegedly threw at Father. When the ring could not be found, the parties made an insurance claim and received $9,000. Father testified at trial that he later learned that Mother had intentionally thrown another ring at him, and then took the valuable ring to New Jersey and pawned it. When [4] Mother was asked about this ring incident at trial, she refused to testify and invoked her Fifth Amendment privilege against self-incrimination.

Dr. Elsbeth Freeman, Ph. D., is a clinical psychologist who evaluated both parties at the Trial Court's request.

Mother's family lives in New Jersey.

Mother would buy things and hide them from Father. According to Father, Mother would make sure she got the mail from the mailbox, and he later learned that she did this so she could hide certain bills. In fact, Mother went so far as to have some of the credit card bills mailed directly to a friend's house so Father would not find out how much credit card debt she had incurred. Mother admitted on cross-examination that Father did not want her to obtain any more [5] credit cards, but she did anyway and charged over $20,000 on these additional credit cards. Mother admitted to having a problem managing money. Mother was fired from two jobs during the marriage, and fired from other jobs before the marriage.

After the parties separated and Father initially moved out of the marital residence, Father requested his clothes, as well as some furniture, sheets, and photographs of the child. When he finally received this furniture, some of it had been ruined. For example, one piece of furniture, which originally had belonged to Father's grandmother, had deep gashes in it. A desk was broken. Father's clothes were ripped and torn. An open bottle of Gold Bond powder had been thrown into a bag containing Father's clothes, ruining those clothes. Inside the furniture, Father found several photographs. There was an Easter family photograph and a wedding photograph, but the photos had been cut up and everyone except Father had been cut out of the pictures. Mother denied damaging the furniture and clothes, but she did admit to cutting up the photographs. According to Father, Mother gave him some sheets, but they were sheets that had been used as drop-cloths when the parties had painted the marital residence. The Trial Court found that Mother was responsible for this damage to Father's property. The Trial Court valued the items that were damaged or not returned to Father at $2,150, and entered a judgment for Father in that amount. The facts certainly do not preponderate against the Trial Court's finding that Mother was responsible for damaging Father's property and the amount of that damage was $2,150. We affirm the judgment to Father in the amount of $2,150.

We next will address whether the Trial Court erred when it denied Mother's motions to recuse. The first motion to recuse was filed in September of 2004. One of Mother's primary complaints was that the Trial Court continued with a "fifty-fifty co-parenting schedule" even though the Trial Court at that time knew "very little about the physical history of the child." Mother also was dissatisfied with the Trial Court because the Trial Court had granted Father's motion for a protective order and request for attorney fees, but denied a similar motion filed by Mother. The Trial Court denied the first motion to recuse, stating the "Court has no bias for or against either party, all rulings having been rooted in the evidence presented at trial ...."

Mother's second motion to recuse was filed in November of 2005, after the trial was over and the Trial Court had issued its memorandum opinion. Again, Mother claimed that the Trial Court was prejudiced against her. Mother claimed the Trial Court made comments which Mother perceived to be demeaning to her and praiseworthy toward Father. Mother further claimed that the fact that the Trial Court ordered her visitation to be supervised was further evidence of the Trial

Footnote 5: Mother had these bills sent to the house of her friend, Allison Miller, who was called as a witness at trial and who confirmed that certain bills were sent to her house.

Court's lack of objectivity. Mother also points to the following comments made by the Trial Court to her attorney when denying the second motion to recuse:

You attack the very essence of a judge's job description and you've done this before. I remember when I was a young judge on the bench you had a case go against you strongly and, you know, it must be because I had some sort of bias...

So when you get an adverse result, don't attack the fact finder. If anything, look at your own job performance. If you need to beat up on somebody, beat up on yourself. Say I could have done this trial better. Somebody's got to be guilty, make yourself guilty, don't make the judge guilty....

When the Trial Court denied Mother's second motion to recuse, the Trial Court made several other observations in addition to those selectively emphasized by Mother. For example, the Trial Court also stated:

Well, Mr. Lockridge, you equate adverse findings by a trial judge with bias, with prejudice.... Now I think that you're old enough and long enough in the tooth to realize that there are clients that don't present as well as other clients and that when you represent clients that don't present as well as other clients, you're likely to get an adverse result... I have bent over backwards in both directions in this case and that memorandum opinion in [this] case is absolutely straightforward.

"[W]hether recusal is warranted is left to the discretion of the trial judge, and such decision will not be reversed absent a clear abuse of discretion on the face of the record." *Bd. of Prof'l Responsibility of the Supreme Court v. Slavin*, 145 S.W.3d 538, 546 (Tenn. 2004). Our Supreme Court in *Slavin* also stated:

Tennessee has also recognized that "the preservation of the public's confidence in judicial neutrality requires not only that the judge be impartial in fact, but also that the judge be perceived to be impartial." *Kinard v. Kinard*, 986 S.W.2d 220, 228 (Tenn. Ct. App. 1998). Thus, recusal is also appropriate "when a person of ordinary prudence in the judge's position, knowing all of the facts known to the judge, would find a reasonable basis for questioning the judge's impartiality." *Davis v. Liberty Mut. Ins. Co.*, 38 S.W.3d at 564-65 (quoting *Alley v. State*, 882 S.W.2d 810, 820 (Tenn. Crim. App. 1994)). "Hence, the test is ultimately an objective one since the appearance of bias is as injurious to the integrity of the judicial system as actual bias." *Id.* We note, however, that the mere fact that a judge has ruled adversely to a party or witness in a prior proceeding is not grounds for recusal. *Id.* *Slavin*, 145 S.W.3d at 548.

Father argues that Mother's motions to recuse were nothing more than "claims that every ruling made by the Trial Court that was not in her favor demonstrated the Trial Court's prejudice ... against her." To be sure, Father was the more successful litigant. However, during the course of this litigation, Mother Filed some motions that were granted and Father filed some motions that were denied. Mother's lack of success primarily can be attributed to the Trial Court's determination that Mother was abusive and that she was not being truthful. The Trial Court went so far as to state that "this is a case, unfortunately, of widely disparate credibility..., and it does not favor [Mother]." The Trial Court provided specific examples of contradictory testimony given by Mother and why the Trial Court believed that testimony was untruthful.

In *Wells v. Tennessee Bd. of Regents*, our Supreme Court observed:

Unlike appellate courts, trial courts are able to observe witnesses as they testify and to assess their demeanor, which best situates trial judges to evaluate witness credibility. *See* *State v. Pruett*, 788 S.W.2d 559, 561 (Tenn. 1990); *Bowman v. Bowman*, 836 S.W.2d 563, 566 (Tenn. Ct. App. 1991). Thus, trial courts are in the most favorable position to resolve factual disputes hinging on credibility determinations. *See* *Tenn-Tex Properties v. Brownell Electro, Inc.*, 778 S.W.2d 423, 425-26 (Tenn. 1989); *Mitchell v. Archibald*, 971 S.W.2d 25, 29 (Tenn. Ct. App. 1998). Accordingly, appellate courts will not re-evaluate a trial judge's assessment of witness credibility absent clear and convincing evidence to the contrary. *See Humphrey v. David Witherspoon, Inc.,* 734 S.W.2d 315, 315-16 (Tenn. 1987); *Bingham v. Dyersburg Fabrics Co., Inc.,* 567 S.W.2d 169, 170 (Tenn. 1978).

Wells v. Tennessee Bd. of Regents, 9 S.W.3d 779, 783 (Tenn. 1999). *See also Lockmiller v. Lockmiller,* No. E2002-02586-COA-R3-CV, 2003 WL 23094418, at *4 (Tenn. Ct. App. Dec. 30, 2003), *no appl. perm. appeal filed* ("The cases are legion that hold a trial court's determinations regarding witness credibility are entitled to great weight on appeal."); *See also McBrayer v. Smitherman-McBrayer,* No. E2006-00040-COA-R3-CV, 2007 WL 187938, at * 5 (Tenn. Ct. App. Jan. 25, 2007), *no appl. perm. appeal filed* (emphasizing the importance of assessing witness credibility when a trial court is making a decree of primary residential status and establishing visitation).

Given the vastly contradictory testimony offered by the parties on various issues, the Trial Court was required to make a credibility determination, and it did just that. There is no clear and convincing evidence that the Trial Court's credibility determination was in error. Keeping the Trial Court's credibility determination in mind, we believe the adverse rulings as to Mother were based not on any prejudice against Mother or her attorney, but rather on a disbelief of her testimony and a conclusion that she was abusive. While the Trial Court's comment made to Mother's attorney concerning an incident between them when the judge "was a young judge on the bench..." was inappropriate, it does not rise to the level of demonstrating any prejudice toward Mother or her attorney. After thoroughly considering all of Mother's various arguments on this issue, we conclude that the Trial Court did not abuse its discretion when it denied Mother's motions to recuse.

The next issue is Mother's claim that the Trial Court erred when it designated Father as the child's primary residential parent. In *Burnett v. Burnett,* No. E2002-01614-COA-R3-CV, 2003 WL 21782290 (Tenn. Ct. App. July 23, 2003), *no appl. perm. appeal filed,* this Court discussed the relevant standard of review in child custody cases. We stated:

The standard of review on appeal for issues addressing child custody and visitation was set forth by our Supreme Court in *Suttles v. Suttles,* 748 S.W.2d 427 (Tenn. 1988), and recently reaffirmed in *Eldridge v. Eldridge,* 42 S.W.3d 82 (Tenn. 2001). In *Suttles,* the Court acknowledged the general rule that:

Although ... "the details of custody and visitation with children are peculiarly within the broad discretion of the trial judge," *Edwards v. Edwards,* 501 S.W.2d 283, 291 (Tenn. App. 1973), and that the trial court's decision will not ordinarily be reversed absent some abuse of that discretion, "in reviewing child custody and visitation cases, we must remember that the welfare of the child has always been the paramount consideration" for the courts. *Luke v. Luke,* 651 S.W.2d 219, 221 (Tenn. 1983)....

Suttles, 748 S.W.2d at 429. The Supreme Court further explained the abuse of discretion standard in *Eldridge,* stating:

Under the abuse of discretion standard, a trial court's ruling "will be upheld so long as reasonable minds can disagree as to propriety of the decision made." *State v. Scott,* 33 S.W.3d 746, 752 (Tenn. 2000); *State v. Gilliland,* 22 S.W.3d 266, 273 (Tenn. 2000). A trial court abuses its discretion only when it "applie[s] an incorrect legal standard, or reache[s] a decision which is against logic or reasoning that cause[s] an injustice to the party complaining." *State v. Shirley,* 6 S.W.3d 243, 247 (Tenn. 1999).

The abuse of discretion standard does not permit the appellate court to substitute its judgment for that of the trial court. *Myint v. Allstate Ins. Co.,* 970 S.W.2d 920, 927 (Tenn. 1998).

Eldridge, 42 S.W.3d at 85.

Burnett, 2003 WL 21782290, at **5, 6.

A list of non-exclusive factors to be considered by the trial court in child custody matters are set forth in Tenn. Code Ann. § 36-6-106(a) (2005) which provides, in relevant part, as follows:

(a) In a suit for annulment, divorce, separate maintenance, or in any other proceeding requiring the court to make a custody determination regarding a minor child, such determination shall be made upon the basis of the best interest of the child. The court shall consider all relevant factors including the following where applicable:

1. The love, affection and emotional ties existing between the parents and child;
2. The disposition of the parents to provide the child with food, clothing, medical care, education and other necessary care and the degree to which a parent has been the primary caregiver;
3. The importance of continuity in the child's life and the length of time the child has lived in a stable, satisfactory environment; ...
4. The stability of the family unit of the parents;
5. The mental and physical health of the parents;
6. The home, school and community record of the child;

* * *

7. Evidence of physical or emotional abuse to the child, to the other parent or to any other person; ...
8. The character and behavior of any other person who resides in or frequents the home of a parent and such person's interactions with the child; and
9. Each parent's past and potential for future performance of parenting responsibilities, including the willingness and ability of each of the parents to facilitate and encourage a close and continuing parent-child relationship between the child and the other parent, consistent with the best interest of the child.

In making its custody determination, the Trial Court discussed the various factors as follows:

[L]et me note that both of these parents demonstrate characteristic one, "love, affection and emotional ties" between themselves and [the child]. As to criteria two, both have the disposition to provide her with food, clothing, medical care and other necessary care. Mother was the primary caregiver when the child was very young. The father has been very active in her life throughout, and when this case began, a 50/50 caretaker of the child. He did well during that period of time, as did mother.... Factor three is not relevant. Factor four is the stability and respective family unit of [the] two parents. This is of limited relevance. The mother appears to have an excellent stepfather; the father has an excellent mother. Factor five is extremely relevant: mental and physical health of respective parents. Factor eight, the evidence of physical or emotional abuse to the other parent, is extremely relevant ... and it reflects very badly on the mother, as does ten, the willingness and ability of each to facilitate and encourage a close and continuing parent/child relationship between the child and the other parent.

The Trial Court properly considered the pertinent statutory factors. Given the evidence contained in the extensive record before us, we conclude that the Trial Court did not abuse its discretion when it determined that, overall, the relevant factors favored Father and that it was in the child's best interest for Father to be the primary residential parent.

The next issue involves the amount of Mother's co-parenting time and the requirement that her visitation be supervised. When the Trial Court initially declared the parties divorced and designated Father as the primary residential parent, Mother was awarded standard co-parenting time which did not have to be supervised. Father filed a post-trial motion seeking to restrict Mother's co-parenting time because, according to Father, his daughter told him "You've been mean to Mommy and stole her house and she has to move far, far away back to New Jersey...." The child apparently made similar comments to her care-giver. Father also claimed:

Since the close of proof in this matter, the Mother has made statements to the Father that cause him continuing concern about the Mother's psychological stability. Specifically, on October 4, 2005, the eve before the Memorandum Opinion was delivered to the parties, the Mother called the Father and told him that she knew where the Father's attorney lived, and knew what color and make of car the Father's attorney's children drove.

Following a hearing on the allegations made by Father in the above motion, the Trial Court credited Father's testimony and reduced Mother's co-parenting time and directed that her co-parenting time be supervised.

Given Mother's behavior throughout the marriage and the course of these proceedings, it certainly is understandable why the Trial Court ruled the way it did. Nevertheless, we believe it is in the best interest of the child for Mother to have more co-parenting time with the child and that her co-parenting time should be unsupervised. We, however, are reluctant to definitively institute such a requirement at this time because this Court does not have before it any proof concerning Mother's post-trial behavior, including additional inappropriate behavior, if any. Therefore, on remand, the Trial Court is instructed to conduct a hearing on this issue. If Mother has not engaged in further inappropriate behavior post-trial which would rise to the level of necessitating that her visitation continue to be supervised, then the Trial Court is instructed to enter an order providing Mother with standard, unsupervised co-parenting time.

The next issue is whether the Trial Court erred when it denied Mother's post-trial motion to have certain property deemed her separate property. Local Rule 10 of the Knox County Fourth Circuit Court provides, in relevant part, as follows:

10. Pre-Trial Stipulations as to Separate and Marital Property. At least forty-eight (48) hours before the day of trial, the parties shall file with the Clerk three (3) JOINTLY EXECUTED AGREED STIPULATIONS as to real and personal property, setting forth, pursuant to the criteria of Tenn. Code Ann. § 36-4-121: (1) the real and personal separate property and debt of each of the parties; (2) the real and personal marital property and debt of the parties; (3) the remaining real and personal property and debt of the parties, the character of which is disputed and to be decided by the Court. This last item consists of all real and personal property and debt of the parties not covered under the first two stipulations.... (emphasis in the original)

The parties complied with this local rule and submitted to the Trial Court a listing of items the parties deemed separate or marital property, along with a listing of disputed items. When the joint stipulation was presented to the Trial Court prior to trial, Father was not living in the marital residence, and Mother was. Following the trial, the Trial Court awarded the marital residence and responsibility for the corresponding three mortgages to Father. There was approximately $27,000 to $28,000 in equity. The Trial Court ordered that the mediator's fees, Dr. Freeman's fees, and the court costs be paid from the equity. The remaining equity was to be divided 50/50 between Mother and Father. Father had two individual retirement accounts with a combined approximate value of [6] $7,370, which the Trial Court divided 50/50. The Trial Court valued Father's interest in a company he operated at $240,000. The Trial Court divided this asset 50/50 and ordered Father to pay Mother $60,000 within 45 days and the remaining $60,000 over the next twelve months at the rate of $5,000 per month. The Trial Court ordered Father to pay additional debt totaling $42,000, which consisted [7] of a Bank of America Visa debt of $21,000, a Chase Visa debt of $12,000, and a debt to a local credit union of $9,000. Mother was ordered to pay approximately $22,900 in various other credit card debt. Mother was awarded as her separate property a ring valued at $15,000.

After the Trial Court classified and divided the most significant items of marital property, divided the marital debt, and classified certain property as separate property of Father or Mother, all of the remaining property was deemed "line item property." The Trial Court instructed the parties to divide this property with Mother making the first selection, then Father making the next selection, and so on and so forth until all of the property was selected. The parties did just that.

Mother filed a post-trial motion claiming that she had neglected to include certain items of her personal property on the Local Rule 10 list of property. As a result, this property was not classified as her separate property because the Trial Court was not aware it existed. Mother claimed these items were gifts from her parents and should have been awarded to her as her separate property. Father claimed some of these items were marital property. The Trial Court denied the motion, stating, *inter alia*, that:

[a]ny separate property or any marital property could have been and should have been stipulated or disclosed. And then we've gone through, disclosed as disputed status property. And we've had a classification argument. We did. These things are simply omitted. And in a case of this length, in particular, that is inexplicable.... At some point, the trial preparation phase ends, and the case goes to trial.

Mother's motion is nothing less than her request to reopen the proof to allow further testimony regarding the items she neglected to include in the Rule 10 list and to reopen the proof regarding how these items should be classified, i.e., as marital or separate property. We will treat

The amount of Mother's share of the equity was to be reduced by the $4,408.43 in attorney fees and expenses

Mother owed Father, any unpaid court costs associated with the order of protection, and the $2,150 judgment against Mother for the destruction of Father's property discussed previously.

The Trial Court entered a post-trial order altering the payment schedule. According to the new order, Father [7] was to pay Mother $30,000 by June 11, 2006, and then no less than $20,000 per year thereafter until the entire $120,000 was paid. Simple interest was to accrue beginning June 11, 2006, at the rate of 7½% per year.

Mother's motion as a Tenn. R. Civ. P. 59.04 motion to alter or amend the judgment. We review a trial court's determination of whether to grant a Rule 59.04 motion to alter or amend a judgment under an abuse of discretion standard. *See Stovall v. Clarke*, 113 S.W.3d 715, 721 (Tenn. 2003). We conclude that the Trial Court did not abuse its discretion when it denied Mother's motion to reopen the proof following a very lengthy trial simply because Mother neglected to include certain items of property on the list as required by Local Rule 10 or because Mother neglected to update that list prior to trial or even any time during this lengthy trial. We note that Mother was living in the house both when the Rule 10 list was submitted to the Trial Court and during the trial. Mother acknowledges in her brief that many of these items were purchased by her parents when her parents were living with her in the marital residence over the summer. Mother has set forth no justifiable reason explaining why she did not include these items on the Local Rule 10 list or why she neglected to update that list before the parties divided the line items. The Trial Court's denial of Mother's motion is, therefore, affirmed.

The next issues surround alimony. The factors to consider when determining whether to award alimony are set forth in Tenn. Code Ann. § 36-5-121(i) (2005), which provides as follows:

1. In determining whether the granting of an order for payment of support and maintenance to a party is

appropriate, and in determining the nature, amount, length of term, and manner of payment, the court shall consider all relevant factors, including:

2. The relative earning capacity, obligations, needs, and financial resources of each party, including income from pension, profit sharing or retirement plans and all other sources;

3. The relative education and training of each party, the ability and opportunity of each party to secure such education and training, and the necessity of a party to secure further education and training to improve such party's earnings capacity to a reasonable level;

4. The duration of the marriage;

5. The age and mental condition of each party;

6. The physical condition of each party, including, but not limited to, physical disability or incapacity due to a chronic debilitating disease;

7. The extent to which it would be undesirable for a party to seek employment outside the home, because such party will be custodian of a minor child of the marriage;

8. The separate assets of each party, both real and personal, tangible and intangible;

9. The provisions made with regard to the marital property, as defined in § 36-4-121;

10. The standard of living of the parties established during the marriage;

11. The extent to which each party has made such tangible and intangible contributions to the marriage as monetary and homemaker contributions, and tangible and intangible contributions by a party to the education, training or increased earning power of the other party;

12. The relative fault of the parties, in cases where the court, in its discretion, deems it appropriate to do so; and

13. Such other factors, including the tax consequences to each party, as are necessary to consider the equities between the parties.

When making its ruling on alimony, the Trial Court discussed the above statute and stated as follows:

There are 12 factors for spousal support. Many of them have been dealt with under equitable distribution [of the marital property.] Some of them have not been spoken to. I would note, again, factor three is relevant; this is a brief marriage. I would note, again, wife's separate assets of $15,000. I would note, again, that the relative fault of the parties applicable to the spousal support statute favors the husband....

This is not a case for any significant spousal support. It is a brief marriage. In no way has the mother impaired her career or ability to make at least $36,000 a year. She has let her college [8] education languish, but that was her own choice. She presents no cogent plan for further education and no proof whatsoever of enhanced earning power through such education. Whether she

The Trial Court noted that Mother's most recent employment was as a catering sales manager making $36,000 [8] annually. When child support was set following the trial, Mother at that time was earning $48,000 per year, which did not include an unidentifiable amount of income as gratuity.

pursues it or not is her choice. The Court accordingly cannot find that the same would enhance her earning power, but who knows what the future holds? She suggests that she should have rehabilitative alimony of $3,000 per month for 48 months to finish her undergraduate education, to start after her daughter begins school. Well, the Court cannot find that rehabilitation is feasible, appropriate or proper, but we do note that there were some payments made upon the husband's student loans during the marriage, education completed before the marriage. Some payments were made upon the husband's student loans during the marriage. I either did not note the amounts, or they did not fall in the testimony, but whatever that amount may be, a judgment for the wife of 50 percent of that number to assist her, if she chooses, in her own education. That number is pronounced as 9 alimony in solido. Given the extreme financial load placed upon [Father] otherwise in this opinion, the payment of that number can be at a schedule far more relaxed than the schedule announced above.

The Court does not find the wife in need of rehabilitation. Indeed, she does not need further education. She earned $36,000 at her last job and was rising in her field of hotel and catering sales when she left her last employment....

Our legislature tells us that transitional alimony is for a determinative period of time, and it is awarded when the Court finds that rehabilitation is not necessary, but the economically disadvantaged spouse needs assistance to adjust to the economic consequences of a divorce, legal separation or other proceeding where spousal support may be awarded. There shall be some transitional alimony addressed below. It is non-modifiable.

The Legislature gives us another option for spousal support, which is called lump sum alimony or alimony in solido; I've spoken to that above. It is the only alimony in solido that will be pronounced in this cause. I touched upon attorney fees. The Court notes that the husband already paid $7,500 as alimony toward wife's attorney fees. Noting that, each party shall hereafter be responsible for the remaining attorney fees that they have incurred.

* * *

This amount of Father's student loan payments made during the marriage was later determined to be $10,395, [9] thereby resulting in a judgment to Mother in the amount of $5,197.50.

It is most painful for this judge to inject yet another negative note in this already sad case, but the Court has already found that the wife has withheld from the husband at separation his clothing, his family furniture, all the contents of the home, save the sheets that were used for painting drop cloths, and maliciously damaged his clothing and furniture before it was finally delivered. She simply cannot be left in the home to serve as a trustee for these items for these two parties. There is substantial furniture and furnishings. She cannot serve as trustee. It would be negligent of this Court to allow that to happen. This Court will not endure any more litigation as to what items were damaged by the wife over the next seven days or what disappeared or what's not there.

Accordingly, she is not to return to the home today .... This is highly irregular, but this case has been highly irregular in every aspect. Her agent or agents shall go to the home today, in the presence of the husband and his counsel, and remove her clothing and uniquely personal effects, as well as 50 percent of all linens and towels. The entire transaction shall be videotaped.... It is to be anticipated that the wife will lodge in a hotel for the next seven nights. The Court directs that the husband shall today book and guarantee payment for seven nights' lodging at the Knoxville Marriott.... This is a non-modifiable incident of transitional alimony.

Tennessee courts have stated on numerous occasions that a trial court has broad discretion in determining the type, amount and duration of alimony, depending on the particular facts of each case. *See, e.g., Wood v. Wood*, No. M2003-00193-COA-R3-CV, 2004 WL 3008875 at *4, (Tenn. Ct. App. Dec. 28, 2004), *app. denied* June 27, 2005 (citing, *inter alia, Burlew v. Burlew*, 40 S.W.3d 465, 470 (Tenn. 2001) and *Sullivan v. Sullivan*, 107 S.W.3d 507, 511 (Tenn. Ct. App. 2002)). Appellate courts are disinclined to second guess a trial court's decision regarding alimony unless it is not supported by the evidence or is contrary to public policies reflected in the applicable statutes. *Nelson v. Nelson*, 106 S.W.3d 20, 23 (Tenn. Ct. App. 2002). "The two most relevant factors in determining the amount of alimony awarded are the economically disadvantaged spouse's need and the obligor spouse's ability to pay." *Broadbent v. Broadbent*, 211 S.W.3d 216, 222 (Tenn. 2006).

The primary problem with Mother's argument on appeal regarding alimony is that she does not set forth what her specific monthly financial obligations are and how much money she needs to meet those obligations. Likewise, she does not set forth what Father's monthly financial obligations are and how much money he has left over each month after meeting those obligations. Because this critical information is not discussed, Mother's brief contains no corresponding citations to the record indicating where this information can be found in the voluminous record on appeal. *See Bean v. Bean*, 40 S.W.3d 52, 55-56 (Tenn. Ct. App. 2000)("Courts have routinely held that the failure to make appropriate references to the record and to cite relevant authority in the argument section of the brief as required by Rule 27(a)(7) constitutes a waiver of the issue.")(citations omitted). Mother simply states that she now has monthly gross income of $4,000, plus an unidentifiable amount of "additional income as gratuity." We know that Father's gross income was substantially more at $12,371.50 per month. However, Father also was held responsible for much more than half of the marital debt. Mother does not discuss how much money, if any, Father is left with after paying the multiple mortgages on the house and the other debt he was ordered to pay, including a substantial amount of credit card debt incurred by Mother during this short duration marriage. In addition, Mother does not explain how her financial need and Father's ability to pay is affected by Father's requirement that he pay her $30,000 by June 11, 2006, and $20,000 per year thereafter until a total of $120,000 is paid, plus interest. In short, we are unable to ascertain whether Mother actually has a need for additional alimony or whether Father has the ability to make such a payment.

Mother also claims the Trial Court erred when it failed to award her any attorney fees over and above the $7,500 that Father was ordered to pay. An award of attorney fees in a divorce case constitutes alimony in solido. *See Herrera v. Herrera*, 944 S.W.2d 379, 390 (Tenn. Ct. App. 1996). Because Mother has not set forth the information necessary for us to ascertain whether additional alimony should have been ordered, we likewise will not disturb the Trial Court's finding on this particular point.

The final two issues are evidentiary. Taken verbatim from Mother's brief, these issue are:

A. Whether it was error for the Court to admit into evidence the report of Dr. Freeman, the Court's own expert witness, as well as her entire office file, when Dr. Freeman was present to testify and did in fact testify at the trial of this matter.

B. Whether it was error for the Court to admit certain hearsay statements of the minor child into evidence and use those statements as grounds for further restriction of the Appellant's co-parenting time.

In *McDaniel v. CSX Transp., Inc.,* 955 S.W.2d 257, 263-64 (Tenn. 1997), our Supreme Court observed that "questions regarding the admissibility, qualifications, relevancy and competency of expert testimony are left to the discretion of the trial court." *Id.* at 263-64 (citations omitted). Thus, a trial court's evidentiary ruling may be reversed only "if the discretion is arbitrarily exercised or abused."

Mother argues that the above evidence should not have been admitted and its improper admission resulted, in part, in her having reduced co-parenting time which had to be supervised. Since we have remanded this case for further proceedings as to Mother's co-parenting time and whether that co-parenting time should be unsupervised, these evidentiary issues are rendered moot. We again emphasize that on remand Mother should be given standard co-parenting time that is not supervised, unless she has engaged in conduct post-trial that rises to the level of necessitating that her co-parenting time remain restricted and supervised.

CONCLUSION

The judgment of the Trial Court is affirmed and this cause is remanded to the Trial Court for further proceedings consistent with this Opinion and for collection of the costs below. Costs on appeal are taxed to the Appellant, Heather L. Rusch-Jones, and her surety.

D. MICHAEL SWINEY, JUDGE

AFTERWORD

Well, you've done it. You have read the whole ball of wax. The Afterword is the place I thank you for the effort you have expended, for the gift you have given of your time. The Afterword is also where the author thanks other persons to whom he is indebted.

I am certainly indebted (as I wrote in my 2017 *Politics, Faith, Love: A Judge's Notes on Things That Matter*) to an unbroken line of great teachers who graced my life: Miss Freeman, who made me cry but taught me seventh grade English at Tyson Junior High; Robert Webb who introduced me to Latin in the ninth grade; Ted Bruning, my English teacher for four years at Webb; B.E Sharp, Webb's teacher of life skills; and John Sobieski, professor of civil procedure at UT Law School. I now add to the list Eugene Rochow, inventor of silly putty and teacher of Chemistry One, and Robert Spaethling, teacher of German A, both of whom I was privileged to have at Harvard my freshman year.

You know that as a part of my excessive education, I have a PhD in Germanic Languages and Literatures. I do not list any Yale PhD instructors among my great teachers.